Grumman F-14
Tomcat

Grumman F-14
Tomcat

107

Doug Richardson

Published in 1985 by Osprey Publishing Limited
12–14 Long Acre, London WC2E 9LP
Member company of the George Philip Group
© Doug Richardson 1985

Sole distributors for the USA

Publishers & Wholesalers Inc
Osceola, Wisconsin 54020, USA

British Library Cataloguing in Publication Data

Richardson, Doug
    Grumman F-14 Tomcat.—(Osprey air combat)
    1. Tomcat (Jet fighter plane)
    I. Title
    623.74'64   UG1242.F5

    ISBN 0-85045-627-4

Editor Dennis Baldry
Filmset in Great Britain by Tameside Filmsetting
Limited, Ashton-under-Lyne, Lancashire and printed
by BAS Printers Limited, Over Wallop, Hampshire

FRONT COVER
*Two F-14A Tomcats of VF-84 'Jolly Rogers' being
readied for flight aboard the USS* Nimitz *(CVN-68) in
January 1983*
(Jean-Pierre Montbazet)

TITLE PAGES
F-14A of VF-74 'Be-Devilers' lined-up on one of
Saratoga's *bow catapults in August 1984*
(Jean-Pierre Montbazet)

Contents

In memory of Cliff Barnet, Stephen Piercey,
Darrell Cornell and Jane Haldane Richardson.

'The stait of man dois change and vary,
now sound, now seik, now blith, now sary,
now dansand mery, now like to dee;
Timor mortis conturbat me.'

(William Dunbar c.1460–c.1513)

Chapter 1
A fighter takes shape

All pilots complain of excessive paperwork, but one document to which Soviet pilots pay zealous attention is the regular intelligence bulletin. And on a spring day in April 1970, one of these reports was troubling MiG-17 trainee Viktor Belenko. Assigned to a training unit near Armavir, he was catching up with the reports of the latest US Navy fighter when the significance of what he was reading hit home. The new fighter which one day he might have to fly against would have a radar range of 180 miles (290 km), and the ability to fire up to six missiles near-simultaneously at targets 100 miles (160 km) away.

This level of performance was far in advance of any Soviet warplane which he might hope to fly. These had a 50 mile (80 km) radar range and missiles of 18 miles (30 km) range. Even if he survived the long-range US missile fire, the US Navy aircraft would still have the ability to outfly in a dogfight any Soviet fighter in the foreseeable future. The young cadet was already nursing doubts concerning the communist system, and the report he was reading did little to dispel them. Six years later, he was to point the nose of a Mikoyan MiG-25 *Foxbat* fighter towards Japan, beginning a flight which was to make newspaper headlines and present the West with a near-new example of *Foxbat*.

The impression which the 1970 incident made on Belenko is obvious from his biography published four years later. The aircraft which so dismayed him to the point where he secretly wondered for the first time why American technology should be superior to its Soviet equivalent was the Grumman F-14 Tomcat—to this day the world's finest long-range interceptor.

Back in the 1950s the US Navy was working with McDonnell on the F4H shipboard interceptor, the aircraft which was to become the best-selling F-4 Phantom, but was already studying concepts for the follow-on project. The Phantom seemed all set to be a winner, but the Navy was becoming increasingly concerned by the threat posed by long-range cruise missiles launched by aircraft or submarines positioned up to 200 miles (320 km) from their target. What the Navy wanted was a fighter able to engage such targets at a range well beyond that of any current air-to-air missile, and having the ability to guide several missiles simultaneously against multiple targets.

One concept which showed promise involved packaging the required interception performance in the missile rather than the aircraft which carried it. This seemed a workable alternative to the traditional carrier-based fighter, so in 1957 the service issued Requests for Proposals to the aircraft and missile industry. In 1959, the Navy launched its Fleet Air Defense Fighter (FADF) programme, ordering the Douglas F6D-1 Missileer and Bendix XAAM-10 Eagle air-to-air missile armament.

In appearance, the Missileer looked more like a bomber than a fighter. This relatively large subsonic aircraft resembled a scaled-up A-6, having a bulbous radar-equipped nose, two-man cockpit with side-by-side seating, a shoulder-mounted unswept wing, and twin engines mounted within the fuselage. Top speed was only Mach 0.8. Instead of engaging in traditional dogfights, the Missileer was intended to remain on patrol for periods of up to six hours, tracking targets at long range using its powerful nose-mounted Hughes pulse-Doppler radar, and engaging threats with Eagle missiles, several of which could be guided at one time against multiple targets. Three rounds would be carried under each wing, plus two more beneath the forward fuselage.

Eagle would have been a massive weapon 16 ft (4.9 m) long and weighing 1,284 lb (852 kg). A solid propellant booster was used in the early stages of flight, with a sustainer taking over the for flight out to targets up to 110 nm (200 km) away. Top speed

would have been Mach 4, the weapon homing in on its target under the guidance of an advanced pulse-Doppler active radar seeker based on that of the Bomarc surface-to-air missile. The warhead could be nuclear or conventional.

At a time when multi-purpose aircraft were considered more attractive than dedicated single-role types, the limitations of the costly and highly specialised F6D were considered unacceptable. Unable to act as a fighter escort for strike aircraft entering hostile airspace, and unable to defend itself once its missile warload had been expended, Missileer was destined never to leave the drawing board, being axed by Defense Secretary Thomas Gates in December 1960. The Eagle missile soon followed Missileer into cancellation, but the concept of using long-range missiles to pick off targets before the latter could close to within range of their own weapons was not forgotten.

With the arrival of a new Administration under President John F Kennedy, a new man took over at the DoD. Robert McNamara came from the Ford Motor Company and was determined to run the Pentagon in a more modern style. He unleashed on the DoD a team of civilian specialists—analysts, engineers, accountants, and lawyers—and started to re-examine many of the current military programmes. McNamara's 'whizz kids' were not content to accept traditional solutions, but demanded that requirements and programmes be justifiable and cost-effective. At the time, this bold approach may have seemed like a good idea, but its wisdom now seems questionable. Programmes such as the B-70 Mach 3 bomber and Skybolt air-launched ballistic missile were ruthlessly axed, while many of the new projects launched under McNamara were to run into cost and technical problems.

For the Navy, one of the serious casualties was the FADF project. The USAF was also looking for a new fighter to replace the Republic F-105 Thunderchief. Specific Operational Requirement 183 called for a tactical fighter able to fly at Mach 2.5 at height, or Mach 1.2 at treetop height, operating out of rough airstrips 3,000 ft (9100 m) long. McNamara reasoned that the two requirements could be merged to create a single Tactical Fighter Experimental (TFX) design which could be deployed by both services. For the

US Navy, the aircraft would carry a Hughes AWG-9 pulse-doppler radar, and an armament of Phoenix missiles, both equipments being based on the technology used in the Missileer and Eagle. The fact that the USAF wanted a strike fighter while the Navy needed an interceptor was ruthlessly brushed aside—the prospect of a dual-role TFX represented savings to the taxpayer of up to a billion dollars, the 'whizz kids' calculated.

The result was to prove a disaster for the Navy. By August 1961, the Secretary of the Navy reported to McNamara that a compromise TFX design could not meet the naval requirement. The Air Force needed a 75,000 lb (34,000 kg) gross weight aircraft, while the Navy required the weight to remain below 50,000 lb (22,700 kg). The size of the lifts on USN carriers created another limitation; total length should not exceed 56 ft (17 m).

McNamara solved the problem by decree. The Navy was ordered to accept a design sized to accommodate a 36 inch radar antenna rather than the 48 inch it required, and to accept a gross take-off weight of 55,000 lb (25,000 kg). Following a design competition between Boeing, General Dynamics, Lockheed, McDonnell Douglas, North American and Republic, McNamara ordered a further evaluation and refinement of the Boeing and GD designs.

Following three rounds of such competitive studies, the Navy still judged the TFX designs unacceptable for carrier use. McNamara ordered a fourth round, then selected not the Boeing design favoured by the services, but the GD submission. The GD bid was more expensive than that from Boeing, but placed greater importance on the commonality favoured by McNamara, who claimed that the USAF and USN versions of the Boeing design had less than 50 per cent commonality in wing, fuselage and tail structure. 'Boeing is in effect proposing two different airplanes', he stated.

GD had teamed with Grumman for the TFX programme. The latter company was to build the aft fuselage and landing gear of all the resulting aircraft, and would assemble and test the naval version. The USAF fighter was designated F-111A, the USN interceptor the F-111B. Instead of the 55,000 lb (25,000 kg) fighter it wanted, the Navy was forced to accept a 63,500 lb (28,800 kg) design.

The resulting saga was a sorry one. The GD aircraft had problems with drag and weight which were to prove fatal for the USN version. Even by the time of first flight, the empty weight of the F-111A had risen by around 15 per cent, from the specified 36,700 lb (16,650 kg) to more than 42,000 lb

OPPOSITE TOP
A long line of Grumman 'Cats' have served with the US Navy, the most famous the F6F Hellcat shown here. More than 12,000 of these tough high-performance fighters were built during WW2 and US and Allied Hellcat units downed more than 6,000 enemy aircraft (US Navy via Robert F Dorr)

OPPOSITE BELOW
The Grumman F11F Tiger was the company's first supersonic naval fighter. It entered service in 1957 but was soon eclipsed by the more successful Vought F-8 Crusader (Robert F Dorr)

OVERLEAF
From the early 1960s onwards, the McDonnell Douglas F-4 Phantom was the yardstick by which supersonic. interceptors were measured—this F-4J is from VF-31, a unit which now flies the Grumman Tomcat (US Navy via Robert F Dorr)

(19,000 kg). The first F-111B flew on 15 May 1965, but had a staggering gross weight of more than 70,000 lb (31,750 kg). Weight was not the only problem. The F-111B was to share the engine and inlet headaches which dogged the F-111A and several subsequent Air Force versions of the GD fighter, and trials soon showed that the high angle of attack and steeply-sloping windshield gave an unacceptable view during carrier-style landings.

In an attempt to contain the weight problem, the F-111B was subjected to a Weight Improvement Programme (WIP), whose effectiveness may be judged by the need for a subsequent Super Weight Improvement Programme, and no less than three Colossal Weight Improvement Programmes! These were not minor modifications and involved radical structural surgery. Commonality and projected cost savings evaporated in the face of these frantic engineering efforts.

In public, Grumman maintained a 'stiff upper lip', arguing that the aircraft's potential should not be

The F-111B was a disaster for the US Navy but its cancellation led to the development of the F-14 Tomcat. These two views of F-111B buno 151972 show the airplane launching an AIM-54 Phoenix missile and (inset) minus AWG-9 radar, being used for TF30 engine testing at NATF Lakehurst, New Jersey, on 29 October 1975 (US Navy/Robert F Dorr)

judged by the prototypes. The company public relations department even issued a document which compared criticism of the F-111B with that directed at the early prototype Phantoms, claiming that like the F-4, the F-111B would eventually be successful. Behind the scenes, however, the company were already studying a possible replacement for the obese F-111B.

If any new design was to meet the US Navy's timescale, it would have to make maximum use of the F-111B and its associated technology and sub-systems. By October 1967, Grumman had drawn up a new proposal which repacked the F-111B avionics and engines within a new swing-wing fuselage which would use more modern engineering methods and

RIGHT
Tomcat as it might have been: when the mock-up of the proposed Grumman 303E fighter was built, the design still featured a single tail fin
(Grumman)

BELOW
Although far from a refined design, configuration 303-60 laid the groundwork for the further studies which would result in the F-14
(Grumman)

larger-scale use of titanium to minimize weight. A second proposal coupled the same airframe and systems with a pair of the new Advanced Technology Engines then under development.

The USN liked what it saw, so Grumman pressed ahead with its studies. By January 1968 it was working on Design 303-60, a twin-engined fighter with a high-mounted variable-sweep wing. Head of the design team was Mike Pelehach, now President of Grumman.

Like the FB-111, Mirage G, Panavia Tornado, MiG-23 *Flogger* and Su-24 *Fencer*, the 303-60 has a high-mounted wing, rather than a low-mounted wing as on the F-4 Phantom. The only fighters to break this rule are the mid-wing Su-17/20/22 series whose wing position was pre-determined by that of their Su-7 ancestor.

High-mounted wings have several advantages over low-mounted wings, even on a fixed-wing fighter. Pylon-mounted stores are at a convenient height which gives good access to armourers and other technicians, while store-to-ground clearance is high, reducing the risk of unexpended stores scraping the ground if the aircraft suffers a wing drop at touchdown.

From the designer's point of view, high wing configurations have another advantage when a VG fighter is wanted. 'In the design of an airplane, the landing gear is fixed relative to where the wing is,' explains Mike Pelehach. 'In fighter airplanes, the gear needs to be near the CG (centre of gravity). The CG is near the centre of lift, which means that it's somewhere near the centre of the wing.' In a low-

wing design the wing box used to carry the pivots and to transfer the loads between fuselage and wing, and the actuators needed to move the wing, would be competing for space within the volume of the inboard fixed wing glove with the undercarriage. 'The fuselage houses all the mechanism for wing actuation—so there's no room to put a gear. The only thing to do is to put the wings on top of the airplane, and put the gear on the bottom.' The glove is thus left free for the wing box and actuators, while the undercarriage can have the space it needs in the lower fuselage. 'A combination of stores clearance and the

OVERLEAF

TOP LEFT
Design 303D was relatively orthodox, with twin engines buried within the fuselage. High drag and excessive fuel consumption put paid to this configuration. Most published accounts state that the 303D had a low-mounted wing, but this model in Grumman's archives shows a high wing (Grumman)

BOTTOM LEFT
VFX-1C was one of the earliest configurations studied by Mike Pelehach's design team. Note the mid-fuselage wing location (Grumman)

TOP RIGHT
In an attempt to reduce costs, single-seat, fixed-wing, and variable-geometry designs were studied (Grumman)

BOTTOM RIGHT
Design 303F explored the possibility of a fixed-wing design (Grumman)

space needed for the landing gear forces you to put the wing either mid or high, but never low.' In larger aircraft such as the B-1, the sheer size of the airframe makes a low wing practical, since the undercarriage can be stowed in secondary structure, but high-wing remains the general rule for fighters.

Outwardly similar to the final F-14, although having a single vertical fin, 303-60 was by no means an optimized design, but did show how a useful fighter might be created. Completed in January 1968, this was compared with the F-111B in a USN study carried out in the spring of that year. This showed the clear superiority of the new proposal over the F-111B, an aircraft which was itself inferior in many respects to the F-4 Phantom it was intended to replace. This was the final nail in the F-111B's coffin. In May 1968 Congress effectively terminated the F-111B programme by the simple act of refusing to fund any further work. Formal cancellation followed in December, but by that time the Navy was already

RIGHT
The mock-up shows how technicians would have good access to the avionics bays
(Grumman)

BELOW
The F-14 Tomcat mock-up, now in the definitive twin-tail form
(Grumman)

hard at work on the planned VFX replacement.

Two months after the Congressional action, the USN issued its VFX specification to the US aerospace industry. Five companies responded with designs, and Grumman found itself in competition against General Dynamics, LTV, McDonnell Douglas, and North American Rockwell. The new requirement called for a fighter able to perform fleet defence, interdiction and ground attack missions. Equipped with the long-range Phoenix missile system, it would provide all-weather protection for carrier battle groups against long-range bomber and cruise missile threats which the Soviet Union might deploy between the mid-1970s and the end of the century.

For the intercept role, the new fighter was to be capable of remaining on patrol 100 or even 200 miles (160–320 km) from a carrier, remaining on station for up to two hours. Phoenix would be the primary long-

OVERLEAF
With its upper section 'mothballed' and its under surfaces metallized, the mock-up was used as a test aid to verify antenna design
(Grumman)

INSET
Grumman technicians prepare to mate a Phoenix missile with the mock-up's weapons pylons
(Grumman)

range armament, with Sparrow being used at shorter ranges. Target performance for the escort/air-superiority role was a radius of action 80 per cent greater than that of the F-4J, plus sufficient fuel for two minutes of combat at maximum afterburner. In the interdiction/close-support role, the new fighter was expected to carry up to 14,500 lb (6600 kg) of low-drag bombs, plus two Sidewinder missiles for self-defence.

Like the F-4 and the now-abandoned F-111B, Tomcat would need a two-man crew to share the workload imposed by the mission and avionics, while naval safety requirements resulted in the use of twin engines. Top speed specified was just over Mach 2.2, allowing the use of conventional aluminium-based alloys.

Conflicting demands such as high speed, high manoeuvrability and good handling at low speeds, virtually dictated the use of variable geometry. A fixed-wing fighter design is at best a compromise, being optimized for one specific combination of speed and altitude. Operating away from this regime—the most likely circumstance for most of any individual sortie—its performance declines accordingly.

Minor modifications to the nacelles of the 303-60 had already resulted in the 303A design, but in order to create a more effective fighter, Grumman engineers launched parallel investigations of three configurations. Further refinement of 303A resulted in 303B, which was evaluated against the other two layouts. Design 303C retained the high variable-geometry wing, but used a more conventional fuselage design with closely-spaced buried engines. It also introduced twin vertical tail surfaces. According to most published accounts, design 303D moved the wing to a low position, buried the engines within the fuselage, and used twin vertical tails. A model in the Grumman archives makes it clear that this design had a *high* wing at one point in its evolution however. Although of vaguely similar configuration to the F-4, 303D proved disappointing. Poor longitudinal stability and drag at subsonic speeds, and excessive fuel consumption in cruise effectively doomed this design, which was dropped in April 1968.

Comparative analysis of the rival B and C versions clearly favoured the B. This offered better perfor-

The copper-plated model was used for RF tests, with millimetre-wave signals playing the role of 'scaled-down' conventional microwave signals (Grumman)

mance in areas such as fuel consumption and supersonic combat ceiling and an engine installation which would be easier to modify in the event of problems, and easier to rework at a later date for new engines. The B was therefore further refined in the late spring and early summer, with the resulting 303E being defined by June.

Back in the late 1960s the F-111 was not the only aircraft with powerplant and inlet problems. In designing the F-14, Grumman was determined to avoid problems with inlets, engines, materials and base drag which had troubled the F-111. Pelehach uses a take-apart wooden model of Tomcat to explain the logic of the configuration. The first step was to avoid the inlet problems which had affected the F-111, especially since the new fighter would use the same powerplant.

'We were looking for an inlet that was not curved—where there was very little distortion.' The solution devised was a powerplant package—a nacelle in which a two-dimensional inlet led the airflow straight back to the engine. 'OK, so we had a nacelle . . . Then we were looking for a body to hang a lot of stores from . . . and we were trying to get the wing pivot further outboard. So we put a wing between the nacelles . . . how far apart we put the nacelles depended on the width that you need to carry two Phoenix with proper clearance.'

It is one thing to read that the centrebody of the F-14 forms more than half of the aircraft's lifting surface, but the components of Pelehach's model make it clear that most of the rear fuselage is a large flat section with an aerofoil-like cross section. With the two model nacelles clipped into place on either side of the flat centre section, and a circular cross-section nose and cockpit section clipped to its leading edge, the result may look like a mutation of Captain James T Kirk's starship *Enterprise*, but the recognizable shape of Tomcat is beginning to form. 'It began to take shape, but there were a lot of considerations given to the location of the wing pivots—both outboard and fore and aft. The F-111 was designed to minimize drag at transonic speeds, but we had a different problem—an airplane which would have long loiter time, also dash capability at altitude . . . The F-14 turned out to be a good looking airplane, but yet it was designed with function in mind.'

While design 303E was being refined, studies of two other configurations explored alternative approaches to the VFX specification. 303F investigated the possibility of using a fixed wing with a double-slotted flap, but analysis soon showed that the larger wing needed for carrier operations imposed a significant weight penalty. Although more than 4,900 lb (2200 kg) heavier than the 303E, it was unable to meet the USN requirement when carrying a full payload of six Phoenix. The addition of a boundary-layer control system would have helped, but additional problems of poor low altitude performance and single-engine rate of climb made the whole concept of a fixed-wing fighter unattractive.

303G was similar in appearance to today's F-14, but slightly smaller. Drawn up to explore the size and weight penalties associated with the large AIM-54 missile, it would have carried the same AWG-10 radar and Sparrow and Sidewinder armament as the F-4 Phantom. It proved a disappointment, being only 1,600 lb (730 kg) lighter than a Phoenix-armed aircraft.

In December 1968 the Grumman and McDonnell Douglas were selected as finalists in the VFX competition. Convinced that it was going to win, Grumman even took the risk of starting work on some components for a 303E prototype. The hard work which had gone into the 303E paid off in the following January, when the Navy selected the Grumman aircraft. It was not the cheapest design offered, but the US Navy judged it to be the best. A contract was awarded to the company on 4 February 1969, while contracts signed in FY71 called for 12 prototypes and 26 production aircraft.

The final design of the F-14 was not frozen until several months after selection of the Grumman design, but was based on the 303E. This already displayed many of the features of the definitive design, such as the large cockpit transparency, horizontal tail surfaces with clipped tips, and a novel system of retractable glove vanes intended to offset the backward movement of the wing centre of lift associated with high angles of wing sweep and with supersonic flight.

One feature which the Navy did not like was the tall vertical fin and folding ventral strake. Although the single fin was lighter than a two-fin design, and offered better performance at high angles of attack, it required the additional area of the strake. Without this, the single tail might have problems in maintaining directional stability in the event of an engine failure at high Mach numbers.

The complexity of the folding strake was considered undesirable for shipboard use, so Grumman switched to a twin tail at the last moment, replacing the large folding strake with two smaller fixed strakes, mounted one beneath each engine nacelle. Although the twin surfaces were heavier than a single tail, it was easier to integrate with the fuselage structure, so the end result was a lighter tail section. Twin tails also gave the aircraft a lower silhouette. Directional control is maintained even under the asymmetric load conditions of missile firing. The twin tails provide sufficient control authority to cope with the failure of one engine at maximum speed, even if one of the stability-augmentation yaw channels has already failed. It should even be possible for a combat-damaged aircraft to return home even after losing a tail. Lower than a single vertical would have been, the twin tails do not require to be folded for hangar storage aboard ship. The two strakes beneath the rear fuselage provide the additional directional stability

required in high-G combat, when the vertical surfaces can become masked by the wing and fuselage. So late in the day was the decision to modify the tail, that the F-14 mock-up was originally displayed with a 303E-style single tail fin.

Having drawn up the 303E and won the contract, Grumman now had the job of translating a paper design into a real aircraft. Construction of sub-assemblies started in late 1968, and the date of first flight was set as on or before 31 January 1971. With the war in Vietnam exposing the dogfight performance limitations of the F-4, the USN wanted its new fighter as quickly as possible.

One aid which greatly speeded the design process was EMMA, the Engineering Mock-up Manufacturing Aid. Mock-ups are normally made from wood and plastic, the constructional method used for the original F-14 mock-up. EMMA was made largely from metal, and could be used as a design aid by the engineers preparing Tomcat's internal 'nerves and sinews'—hydraulic lines, electrical wiring, and power control systems. Back in 1969, mock-up manager Tony Stanziale explained EMMA's purpose in life. 'You might say she's half-way between a wooden mock-up and an actual airplane. Already she is helping to save time . . . and EMMA will cut costs too, by helping to eliminate early production and tooling errors.'

Since EMMA would never fly, her mechanical structure—although accurate in shape and contour—did not need to be manufactured to aerospace standards. Instead of being milled from aluminium, (a process which would have involved three or five months from ordering to delivery) her bulkheads were sand-cast from aluminium in a matter of weeks by a local foundry. EMMA was accurate enough to allow engineers to check the mating and alignment of modular sections and sub-assemblies. Bulkheads, beam hatches and engine mountings were all faithfully reproduced, and EMMA was even strong enough to be used for fit checks of the TF30 turbofans. Having no external skin, EMMA gave engineers good access to her interior. Once successfully installed, wiring harnesses were stripped out and used as a master pattern for production purposes. If the cable fitted EMMA, it would fit the real aircraft.

A top speed of Mach 2.4 imposed no particular problem with materials, allowing conventional aluminium alloys to be used for much of the structure. About 40 per cent of the aircraft is made from aluminium alloy, while around 18 per cent is

This fatigue test rig was used to prove the strength of the F-14 design. The curved track to the right allowed the rig to cope with different wing angles, and the entire experiment was controlled and monitored by the electronic racks in the foreground (Grumman)

made from steel. In order to keep the weight down, a much higher proportion of titanium alloy is used than on earlier fighters, plus composite materials such as boron epoxy.

Stronger than steel, but significantly lighter, titanium is a difficult material to work. Earlier aircraft such as the F-4 Phantom used only limited amounts of titanium, reserving the material for areas of high thermal or physical stress. On the F-4, titanium accounted for only 9 per cent of the structure, but on Tomcat makes up around 25 per cent of the empty weight. It is used for the wing box, wing pivots, wing upper and lower skins, the intakes, rear fuselage skins as well as the hydraulic lines.

On a variable geometry aircraft, wing loads are transferred to the fuselage via the wing pivots and wing box, so the design of these components is critical. When the F-111 wing box was designed in the early 1960s, the designers opted to use a bolt-assembled component manufactured from D6AC steel. Similar constructional methods could have been used for the F-14, but would have posed significant cost and weight penalties. In a bold move, Grumman designers decided to use titanium, and to assemble the wing box by electron-beam welding.

Since the early 1960s the company's engineers had been experimenting with electron-beam welding of titanium and other materials. Using a small vacuum chamber, they had discovered that thick sections of

Pratt & Whitney TF30 afterburning turbofans are prepared for installation in Tomcat (Grumman)

6A1-4V titanium could be welded with a minimum of distortion. Conventional welding operations on thick sections of material demand multiple passes and subsequent inspections, but a single pass would suffice for EB welded titanium.

By 1968 an experimental box-beam structure had been designed, built, and tested to destruction. Typical of a wing box structure, this component coped with all design loads—failure was finally induced by continuing the tests at a 112 per cent load factor. The new welding technique passed this severe test with flying colours. When the test box finally broke, the failure occurred not at a weld but at a tooling mark in the lower cover. This valuable experience was gained just in time to give Grumman the confidence to use an electron-beam welded wing box in its VFX proposal, and on the subsequent F-14 design.

Design of a wing box for any VG aircraft poses severe engineering problems. For a start, the moving outer wing sections transmit large and variable bending and torsional moments as wing angle is varied. The wing/fuselage pivots must be positioned to minimize adverse pitching moments, particularly at high altitudes and high turn rates. The wing box used to carry these pivots is located at the point on the aircraft where cross-section is greatest, forcing the designer to shape the wing box to follow the contours dictated by features such as air-intake ducting.

In the case of the F-14, these factors resulted in a 20 ft long component which also serves as a fuel tank. Its gull-like shape recalls the wing shape of the piston-engined Corsair of World War 2 fame. Fully assembled, it is 22 ft (6.7 m) long, 33–36 inch (83–91 cm) wide, and 14 inch (36 cm) deep. Welded from titanium, the latter is built from a total of 33 separate components. The resulting weight savings were significant—not only was there a direct saving of 900 lb (408 kg) on the box structure itself, but the resulting savings in fuel and structure shaved more

than 22,000 lb (1000 kg) off the Tomcat's gross take-off weight. Each wing mates with the pivots via two sets of lugs. One lug of any two may fail without endangering the aircraft.

The F-111 had pioneered variable-geometry wings, and several were lost following failures of the steel wing box. In order to make sure that this did not happen to the F-14, Grumman subjected the titanium box to a punishing series of tests. By December 1971 fatigue testing of a production-

Despite years of operational experience and many hours of running on the test stand, the Pratt & Whitney TF30 has remained a temperamental powerplant
(Pratt & Whitney)

ABOVE
Technicians prepare a cockpit mock-up for ejection-seat tests (see page 121)
(Grumman)

RIGHT
First of the many—the fuselage of the first prototype starts the journey by road from Grumman's Bethpage works to the Calverton flight-test facility
(Grumman)

standard wing box was completed, the assembly passing the 12,000 hour (2 × service life) design requirement, and being installed in a structural-test airframe for further 'torture'.

The pivot structure achieved the same 12,000 hours goal, then continued to clock up 23,760 hour (almost four times its design life) before failing in March 1971. Its fatigue cracks were repaired, and it then underwent a static load test, failing at 120 per cent of the design ultimate load.

The moving section of the wing incorporates plain trailing-edge flaps, full-span leading-edge slats, lift dumpers, and spoilers. When the wing is in the fully-forward position, the latter act in conjunction with the horizontal stabilizers in order to maintain roll control. Early variable-geometry aircraft used manually-controlled wings, but the F-14 was the first to rely on an automatic system. As Mach number

varies, the air-data computer automatically moves the wing to the position which will give the optimum lift/drag ratio.

Wing sweep may be varied from 20 to 68 degrees, but a special 75 degree position which overlaps the tailplane is provided for use on the ground in order to minimize parking space. Sweep angle is automatically controlled by the air-data computer, in order to optimize the lift/drag ratio. This is particularly effective between Mach 0.6 and 0.9, the range of speeds most likely to be met in air-to-air combat. To improve combat manoeuvrability, the slats and outboard flap sections may be deployed while the wing is in the fully-forward position.

To maintain a smooth fit between the trailing edge of the wing and the upper surface of the rear fuselage, the latter incorporates inflatable canvas bags in its upper surface. These are pressurized with air from

the twelfth stage of the TF30 via a regulator. Teflon paint on the underside of the wing prevents abrasion of the bags.

Two small triangular-shaped vanes are mounted in the leading edge of the gloves. Normally carried in the fully-retracted position, these are extended at supersonic speeds under the control of the air-data computer. Maximum extension is 15 degrees. When extended, these generate additional lift ahead of the aircraft's centre of gravity.

This results in several gains. The extra lift helps to compensate for the nose-down pitching moment which occurs at supersonic speeds, reducing pitch-trim drag, while maintaining manoeuverability by overcoming the sluggishness in pitch control which

would otherwise be experienced. It also offloads the rear fuselage and horizontal stabilizer, reducing the bending stresses on the rear fuselage. As a result, the structure of the aircraft is lighter than would have been possible with a vaneless design. Torsional loads on the wing pivots are also reduced.

All these advantages are purchased at the cost of increased weight and complexity. 'The whole concept of having the vanes is a good one,' says Mike Pelehach, 'but what does it really cost you to fit the associated mechanism and interlocks? Those got a lot more complicated and heavier and more costly than we had envisaged initially. The airplane is designed for Mach 2.4, but we found that in many cases it's an academic number. People don't fly the airplane at 2.4.

The faster you move, the more the lift moves back on the wing, and it really moves back at the last two-tenths of a Mach number. At Mach 2.25 the need for the vanes gets to be marginal. For what the airplane was designed to do, vanes made it better, but was it worth the penalty?

'If I had to do the F-14 all over again, would I put the winglets on the airplane? I don't really know. Would I put something on? Yes, I think I would. I think there are ways of putting a fixed surface on an airplane. Working perhaps in conjunction with a votex, this could be arranged to provide the extra lift when required,' Pelehach explains.

No ailerons are fitted. Roll control is by means of wing-mounted spoilers and the differentially moving tailplane. The wing spoilers are locked down at sweep angles of greater than 57 degrees, leaving control to the horizontal stabilizers. These were the first load-bearing structures in a Western military aircraft to be made from composite materials. Having gained experience with boron epoxy structure by flight testing limited components on the F-111 and A-6, Grumman started development of the F-14A stabilizers in 1968. By 1970 the resulting structures had completed demonstration fatigue and static-load tests, and the Grumman engineers stopped playing 'Mr Nice Guy' with the test specimens.

Tests were carried out at four times ultimate load conditions, then at a temperature of 300 degrees C. The surface under test finally failed at 109 per cent ultimate design loading and at 300 degrees C. The 12,000 hour mark was passed in fatigue testing in September 1971. Testing was continued at 125 per cent loads until the structure used to support the stabilizer finally failed in October 1970 having demonstrated a total fatigue life of more than 24,000 hours.

In designing the F-14 engine installation, Grumman was able to draw on experience gained as far back as 1966, when the company undertook a series of wind tunnel studies of advanced inlet and ejector designs as part of an F-111B improvement programme. The two engines are installed within nacelles located as far apart as possible on the rear fuselage. On fighters with conventional fuselage-mounted intakes, a system has to be devised to divert turbulent boundary air, preventing it from reaching the engines. In the case of the F-111, this is particularly complex, since the intake ducting was

TOP
Late in the afternoon of 21 December 1970, and more than a month ahead of schedule, Grumman chief test pilot Robert Smythe and project pilot 'Bob' Millar taxi out to the runway for Tomcat's first flight
(US Navy via Robert F Dorr)

BOTTOM
The prototype lifts off from the Calverton runway for the first time
(US Navy via Robert F Dorr)

short and the TF30 was prone to stall. Since the F-14 engine nacelles are positioned well out from the fuselage, the inlets run little risk of ingesting boundary layer turbulence. The variable-geometry intakes are of multi-ramp wedge configuration and offer a straight path for the incoming air. This simple scheme avoided the complex intake/inlet interface problems which have dogged the TF30-powered F-111.

Hydraulic actuators fitted in the upper part of the intake adjust the positions of the first and second ramps in the upper surface of inlet and the diffuser ramp located further aft, reducing the inlet air to subsonic velocity and optimizing the airflow to the engine. A gap between the back edge of the second ramp and the leading edge of the diffuser ramp allows bleed air to escape from the inlet, passing overboard via a bleed-air door in the outer surface of the inlet. The Inlet Control Computers operate continuously, calculating the optimum position for the inlet ramps 40 times per second based on parameters such as engine speed, air temperature and pressure, and the aircraft's angle of attack.

The intake design has stood the test of time. The only significant modification has been the deletion of the variable-position feature of the bleed-air door. This was originally of variable area, but experience showed that the actuator could be replaced by a simple mechanical link which held the door in a position giving 100 inch² (645 cm²) of exit area.

Tomcat and the Pratt & Whitney TF30 turbofan were to have a long and controversial career. Privately developed from 1958 onwards as a private-venture civil engine designated JTF10A, this high-compression, axial-flow, twin-spool turbofan failed to attract civil applications, despite the availability of six versions. Notwithstanding this early failure, the new powerplant made significant technological progress, being the first Western turbofan to be equipped with an afterburner, and probably the first in the world.

In the mid-1960s the TF30 was adopted in afterburning form to power the General Dynamics F-111 fighter-bomber. Flight trials started in 1965 in order to qualify the engine for supersonic operation at sea level—a task never before attempted by US engine designers. Early R&D models and the first five production examples of the GD swing-wing fighter were powered by the pre-production TF30-P-1 which developed 18,500 lb (8400 kg) of afterburning thrust. This also powered the first five examples of the F-111B interceptor. Flight-test experience led to modifications to the compressor blades and interstage bleeding. These were incorporated into the production-standard TF30-P-3A of similar rating, which powered the F-111A, -111E, and the Royal Australian Air Force F-111C.

Definitive powerplant for early F-111B interceptors would have been the TF30-P-12, an uprated version of the Air Force's TF30-P-3.

Developing 20,000 lb (9070 kg) with afterburner, this was installed in only two F-111Bs. Although the F-111B was never to see USN service, development of improved TF30s continued for the USAF, with the USN powerplant providing the basis for the later TF30-P-7 and TF30-P-412. For Strategic Air Command's fleet of FB-111A bombers, P&W devised the uprated TF30-P-7, developing around 21,000 lb (9525 kg) with afterburner. The F-111D and F-111F were also fitted with new engines based on the USN TF30-P-12. The F-111D uses the 19,600 lb (8890 kg) TF30-P-9, while the F-111F is fitted with the 25,100 lb (11,385 kg) thrust TF30-P-100. Developed from the -12, this engine is probably the most advanced TF30 production variant and was available from 1971 onwards.

For the Tomcat, the US Navy again turned to the TF30, at least in the short term. Under the original plan, this engine would have powered the prototype, trials and evaluation aircraft, plus the first 67 production examples. Production was then due to switch to the definitive P&W F401 turbofan. As a basis for the Tomcat engine, P&W again used the TF30-P-12 from the F-111B as a baseline. First TF30-P-412 engines for the F-14A were delivered in 1970. These were soon replaced by the improved 20,900 lb (9480 kg) TF30-P-412A, which features a revised afterburner nozzle.

The basic design of the TF30 has been largely unchanged by development work. The annular intake is made from a single-piece casting and leads directly to a three-stage titanium fan mounted within a steel containment case. Located at the forward end of the low-pressure compressor shaft, this has a pressure ratio of greater than 2.1 and a bypass ratio of 0.91 to 1. The remaining six stages on the LP spool are those of the LP compressor, whose titanium rotor blades operate in conjunction with steel stator blades. (Earlier engines such as the P-8 and P-408 have one extra LP stage.)

A seven-stage high-pressure (HP) compressor made from nickel-based alloy offers a further pressure ratio of around 18 to 1, delivering its airflow into eight Hastelloy X annular chambers. The TF30 can burn JP-4 or JP-5 fuel, which is fed to the four fuel nozzles in each chamber by a Chandler Evans two-stage fuel pump.

Hot gas from the chambers is passed to a single-stage HP turbine with air-cooled cobalt-alloy blades, then to a three-stage uncooled LP turbine with nickel-alloy blades. The two-piece turbine casing is of steel construction. Final engine section is the five-zone afterburner, which ends in a variable-area convergent/divergent nozzle. The engine is started by an AiResearch ARS100 air turbine starter. This is located on the left forward drive pod of the accessory gearbox.

Despite the TF30's record of problems, it was the best available engine at the time. More than 3,000 have been delivered over a production run of more than 17 years, so the P&W powerplant can easily claim to be the most widely-used Western after-burning turbofan. Despite its acknowledged deficiencies—largely a result of the age of the basic design—it must be considered a success.

Engine/inlet compatibility testing started in 1969, the results being used to refine the inlet configuration and to establish the control schedule for the variable inlet ramp and exit door. With the demands of the F401 engine in mind, Grumman designed the inlet system to cope with airflows of up to 270 lb/sec (122 kg/sec). In February 1970, an inlet was delivered to Pratt & Whitney for compatibility testing with the F401 engine planned for the follow-on F-14B, and later that year tests with the prototype TF30-P-412 engine cleared the intake and powerplant for the initial flight-test programme.

Flight controls and hydraulics also had to be proved before first flight. The test stand used for this

30 December 1982: the first prototype during its second and final flight. For this sortie, Smythe and Millar changed places, with Millar taking over the front seat (Grumman)

work was made from structural steel, but located all components in the position which they would occupy on the real aircraft. Critical structural inertias and the stiffness of various flight-control surfaces and their attachments were also faithfully reproduced. Into this rig went much of the hydraulic lines, connectors, reservoirs and other components of the hydraulic system, plus the major items of electronics which would interface with the various mechanisms—avionics units such as the Auto-Flight Control System, Central Air Data Computer, Auto-Inlet Control System, Approach Power Compensator and Mach Sweep Programmer. The avionics units and the simulated aerodynamic loading on the flight control surfaces were all programmed via an analogue computer which formed part of the simulator facility.

Operation of the fuel system was checked out on another test rig. This duplicated the aircraft fuel system, and contained the tanks, pumps, valves, and connecting lines. This checked the performance of the system during fuelling, defuelling, engine-feed and fuel-transfer operations, fuel jettison, and the effects on aircraft CG position due to fuel consumption.

Internal fuel capacity is 16,200 lb (7350 kg). Tanks are located in the moving section of each wing, aft of the cockpit, between the engines, and outboard of the engine nacelles. The port wing tank, port side wing box tank and all tanks aft of the wing box (except for the vent tank) feed the port engine, while the starboard wing and wing box tanks plus all tanks ahead of the wing box feed the starboard engine. An additional 3,600 lb (1630 kg) of fuel can be carried externally, bringing the total capacity to 19,800 lb (8980 kg). Wing fuel has a significant effect on aircraft centre of gravity as wing sweep is varied, and the integral tank had to be strong enough to cope with the loads caused by fuel sloshing around during catapult take-off and extreme rolling manoeuvres.

Other specialized test rigs tested the environmental control system, reproducing the cockpit and avionics areas. Tests confirmed the performance of the cockpit air conditioning, canopy demisting system, air-blast rain removal nozzle, windshield anti-icing, and the

When this photograph was taken by a chase aircraft, the trail streaming back from the aircraft was probably fuel being released in a test of the jettison system. A similar trail noted about half an hour after take-off was the first evidence that hydraulic fluid was leaking from the aircraft (Grumman)

each engine. Either can supply all the 115/200 volt (400 Hz) power needed by the aircraft systems. In the unlikely event of both failing, a hydraulically-driven 5 KVA emergency generator can provide enough power to allow the aircraft to abort its sortie, jettison stores, return to base and land.

As the first aircraft took shape, the programme came under a fresh assault—the era of the 'whizz kids' and commonality were not over. Calculating that the Grumman warplane could be out-manoeuvred by a MiG-21, civilian DoD analysts argued that the US Navy needed a higher-performance aircraft, and suggested that a derivative of the USAF's McDonnell Douglas F-15 Eagle be adopted. The USN had had enough commonality for one decade, and backed up by Defense Secretary Melvin Laird, doggedly insisted on the F-14.

As the programme gathered momentum, engineers found ways of speeding the work. When the RF engineering department needed a mock-up for avionics antenna testing, engineering mock-up manager John Arlin pressganged the original mock-up from Plant 1 into fresh service. If the antennas were to behave correctly, they had to be mounted in a mock-up whose skin would conduct electricity. The RF trials would take place out of doors, so the mock-up was given a heavy protective coating, then its upper surfaces were given a layer of the white compound used by the Navy's 'mothball' fleet. The underside was then spray coated with hot zinc, then with tin and copper, making it electrically conductive. During the summer and autumn, the modified mock-up was positioned outdoors, while engineers measured and tested the performance of the antennas associated with the Phoenix and Sparrow missiles and the F-14 avionics. Once the tests were over, back to Plant 1 the mock-up went, so that the mothballing could be stripped off and equipment installed for initial evaluation of the exterior lighting.

One of the final parts of the aircraft to be tested before first flight of the prototype Tomcat was the escape system. Martin-Baker carried out more than 22 flight tests and ground tests of Tomcat's GRU-7A rocket-powered ejection seat, while ejection flight tests from an F-106 and parachute bailouts from an A-3 were conducted at the Naval Air Recovery Facility at El Centro in California to establish seat ejection trajectory and parachute-opening characteristics. Early in December 1970, an F-14 cockpit section containing all systems and components including the ejection seats, canopy system, escape-

liquid cooling system which would be used to control the temperature of the Phoenix missiles.

Tomcat has two main hydraulic systems, the pumps being mechanically driven by the engine power take-off. Should both fail, a self-contained back-up system energized by two electrically-driven pumps can take over. This has enough capacity to allow the aircraft to be flown and landed.

The aircraft has two 60/75 KVA electrical generators, one coupled to the power take-off shaft on

mode selection and pyrotechnic initiation systems was mounted on a rocket-powered sled and blasted down the test track at the Naval Weapons Center, China Lake, at speeds of between 100 and 600 knots (180–1100 km/h). Fitted with instrumented dummies, the seats were ejected, proving that the system would function correctly. What the test crew didn't realize was that within weeks, the seats would be put to the ultimate test.

Just before four o'clock on the morning of Sunday, 25 October 1970, Grumman vice-president Tom Rozzi drove out of Plant 1 at Bethpage. Behind him in another car came Tom Johnson (another company VIP) and behind him a large shrouded shape on a custom-designed flatbed trailer. The first Tomcat was on its way to Grumman's flight test centre at Calverton.

Once safely delivered to Calverton's Plant 7, the aircraft was finally assembled, then put through ground vibration tests, a fuel function check, and calibration. Taxi trials started on 14 December 1970, and by the 21st Tomcat was ready to fly. Despite poor weather, Grumman chief test pilot Robert Smythe and project test pilot William 'Bob' Millar decided to attempt a short flight. With its wings fixed in the forward position, and carrying four dummy Sparrow missiles, the aircraft set off down the Calverton runway just after four o'clock in the afternoon, taking to the air more than a month ahead of the contracted date. Sunset was less than half an hour away, so Smythe cut the afterburner just after take-off, flew two low-speed circuits of the field at 3,000 ft (900 m), then came in to land. The triumphant 'Grummanites' turned their thoughts to Christmas, content to leave the start of detailed testing until after the holiday.

Eight days later on 30 December, Tomcat lifted off the Calverton runway at 10.18. Smythe, who had been in the front cockpit on 21 December, now rode in the rear seat, while Miller sat in front. Accompanied by chase planes, it turned towards the southeast to reach its assigned flight-test area. Stability and control checks went smoothly, the landing gear was retracted, and Miller started to build up the speed from just over 130 knots (245 km/h) to 180 knots (330 km/h). At around 10.43 one of the chase planes noted what appeared to be a trail of smoke leaving the Tomcat.

As the chase plane closed in to take a closer look, Miller reported a primary hydraulic system failure. Aborting the sortie, he turned for home. Although the route back to Calverton took the Tomcat past a small airfield, this had no crash equipment or arrester gear, and the wind was blowing across the runway. Several years later, Smythe was to tell Arthur Reed,

Millar heads the aircraft back towards the coast of Long Island. The sortie was to end with a crash just short of Calverton Field
(Grumman)

air correspondent of *The Times*, 'I remember thinking, I hope we won't regret passing an airfield.'

When four miles (6 km) from Calverton Field, the crew used the emergency nitrogen bottle to blow down the gear. Just after the crew confirmed that it was down and locked, the unthinkable happened—the secondary hydraulic system also failed. Relying on the Combat Survival System, a last-ditch control system driven by an electrical pump and used to operate the rudders and tailerons only, Miller tried to continue the approach and land the aircraft. On the final approach, even this limited control system showed signs of failing. The Tomcat began a gentle longitudinal oscillation which persuaded its crew that their luck had finally run out.

Smythe ejected with the aircraft a bare 25 ft (8 m) above the trees, and the aircraft immediately pitched over into a dive. Miller ejected less than half a second before impact, but like Smythe suffered only superfical injury. Within half an hour, both men were back in the control tower, where their wives and families—VIP guests for the day—had been helpless witnesses of the crash. Since their injuries were confined to a skinned fingertip and a cricked back, both men were able to continue as Tomcat test pilots, but Miller died 18 months later in another Tomcat crash.

An official investigation soon showed that fatigue failures of the pipes in both hydraulic systems had led to a partial failure of the flying controls. In theory, the chances of such a double failure were remote. During the Vietnam war such double failures were not uncommon, but were the result of combat damage. In aircraft such as the F-105, primary and secondary hydraulics were often so close together that the combat damage which knocked one out also wrecked the other. In aircraft such as the Tomcat, the two hydraulic systems were widely separated, a wise move but one which contained the seeds of the prototype's destruction.

The hydraulic system of the Tomcat had to cope with the task of swinging the wings, and was by far the most powerful that Grumman had designed (with the exception of the system devised for the supersonic transport, or SST). Pelehach's team were faced with a very high weight of hydraulics, so opted to use technology developed when Grumman tackled the daunting task of designing NASA's Apollo LEM manned lunar lander. Lightweight titanium hydraulic lines were used, but connected in a novel manner. Conventional hydraulic lines are connected using screw-threaded valves, components which are bulky and prone to leakage. For Tomcat the pipes to be mated were joined using a bimetal sleeve which had been chilled in liquid helium before installation. As the sleeves returned to normal temperature, it shrunk, gripping the lines in a leakproof junction. What was not appreciated was that the new titanium pipework was sensitive to how it was mounted within the aircraft, both in terms of how it is fixed to the fuselage structure and in terms of the distance between fixings.

'What happened was that we had a nine-cylinder hydraulic pump which worked off the engine', recalls Pelehach. 'When we ran the engine and ran the pump—no problems at all. When they flew the airplane ... they were checking single-engine performance. Now you don't shut the engine off, you simply idle the engine.' Here lay the million-to-one chance which was to down the prototype. 'When he (Miller) pulled the engine to idle RPM in flight, that precise RPM of the engine and the nine-cylinder pump happened to be on the frequency that made the lines break.' Faced with vibrations at the exact frequency at which the lines would naturally resonate, the pipework had vibrated, developed metal fatigue and broke.

'When we finally found out what had happened, we put an airplane on a test stand and put the engine to flight idle and watched the pipe—and in nine seconds the pipe broke!' In the case of Tomcat No 1, the second hydraulic system should have allowed the aircraft to continue flying and land safely back at Calverton, but this too had failed. 'We'd put the two systems in the airplane as mirror images, so what broke one side also broke the other.' Primary and secondary hydraulic lines in aircraft built since then take advantage of a rule devised in the light of the 30 December crash—'Hydraulic lines in airplanes must be mounted differently—don't make them mirror images.'

The original prototype had been intended for envelope-expansion flights and high-speed testing, so it carried different instrumentation to those immediately due to follow it. The 12th airframe was renumbered 1X and assigned to these tasks, while work moved ahead on completing the No 2 Tomcat so that flight testing could resume. The US Navy ordered the removal of the titanium hydraulic lines, but the shrink-sleeve fitting method has been retained to the present day. Shortly after discussing the crash with Pelehach, the author was shown similar fittings within the equipment bays of the nearly-completed second X-29 forward-swept wing demonstrator.

On 24 May 1971, five and a half months after the crash, the second prototype took to the air, with Smythe at the controls. A total of 19 aircraft were assigned to flight trials, each being assigned a specific role. The No 2 aircraft was designed for low-speed, high-lift and stall/spin tests. For these tasks, it flew with its wings locked in the 20 degree (fully-open) position, and the air intakes locked in the fully-open configuration. To reduce the risk of low-speed testing, this aircraft was fitted with a 22 ft (6.7 m) diameter stall/spin parachute located on the rear fuselage, and suitable for deployment at speeds of between 120–170 knots (220–315 km/h). Also installed on this aircraft was a Sunstrand hydrazine-powered hydraulic pump. Intended as a back-up system capable of running the flight controls and an

emergency electrical generator, this was a precaution against the possible loss of both engines at low airspeeds, high angles of attack, or spins.

To clear the airframe up to the specified G-loading, the third prototype was flown at progressively increasing airspeeds and loadings. Under the original plan to use Tomcat in the ground-attack role, the aircraft was to have been cleared to 7.5G, but the less demanding interceptor role required only 6.5G clearance.

First aircraft to leave Grumman was the 4th prototype. In October 1971 this was delivered to Point Mugu, California, so that Hughes Aircraft could install the AWG-9 fire-control system and AIM-54 Phoenix missiles. Also delivered to Pt. Mugu were the 5th aircraft (used for systems-installation, test and compatibility work), and the 6th (used for missile-separation and weapon-system compatibility work).

The F-14A was originally planned as an interim aircraft. Production was to have been switched in the early 1970s to the F-14B version. Equipped with the same avionics and weaponry as the -14A, this was to

have been powered by the Pratt & Whitney F401 turbofan.

A result of the Advanced Technology Engine (ATE) programme, the Pratt & Whitney JTF22 demonstrator turbofan engine was developed into two versions, the F100 for the USAF's F-15 Eagle (later adopted for the F-16), and the F401 for use in later-production Tomcats. The Navy engine used the same core section as the F100, coupled to a larger fan and afterburner. The fan on the F100 has three stages, but the F401 added a fourth intermediate-pressure single stage section designed to supercharge the core.

These modifications made the F401 larger than the F100—50.5 inch (128 cm) in diameter rather than 46.5 inch (118 cm), and increased the dry weight from

3,020 lb (1370 kg) to 3,650 lb (1655 kg). Bypass ratio rose from 0.6 to 1 to 0.65 to 1. Maximum dry thrust was 16,400 lb (7440 kg), well above the 14,375 lb (6520 kg) of the USAF engine, while thrust in full afterburner was 28,090 lb (12,740 kg) compared with the 23,810 lb (10,800 kg) of the F100. The twin-engined F-14B would thus have 16,000 lb (7260 kg) more thrust than the basic F-14A, raising the thrust-to-weight ratio from around 0.75 to 1 to more than 1 to 1. Specific fuel consumption of the USN engine was 0.62 lb/lb/hr dry, rising to 2.45 lb/lb/hr in afterburner, figures showing an improvement of nine and four per cent respectively over the F100.

The first engine ran in September 1972, and was flight tested in the F-14B prototype. Initially flown with two TF30 engines, the 7th aircraft was assigned to flight test the F401 engine. Delivery of the Pratt & Whitney engine was delayed, the aircraft finally flying on 12 September 1973 with one TF30 and one F401.

The F100 was already pushing engine technology to the limits, as the early problems with this engine were to demonstrate, but the F401 attempted even more ambitious performance goals. Like the F100, it experienced technical problems, failing its pre-liminary flight-rating tests in 1975. The USAF had no other choice but to stick with the F100, but when the F401 programme got bogged down the US Navy decided to stay with the TF30, cancelling the newer engine and plans to build around 400 F-14Bs. Work on the F401 was finally suspended in April 1974. After the F401 trials, the No 7 prototype was put into storage, and was later reactivated for use as an F101 DFE testbed, and later as an F-14D trials aircraft.

Tasked with avionics-test duties, aircraft No 9 served at Point Mugu for AWG-9 evaluation work. It was joined by No 11, an aircraft used for non-weapon systems-compatibility work. After delivery to the USN's Air Test Center at Patuxent River, the 10th aircraft was used by Grumman for structural validation tests, then taken on board a carrier for catapult-launch and arrested-landing trials. On 30 June 1972, it struck the water while Bob Miller—the pilot who had flown the original prototype on its second and final flight—was practising for a Tomcat demonstration planned for a charity air show at Patuxent Naval Air Test Center. Miller was flying alone, and died in the crash.

By mounting the 13th prototype within an anechoic chamber, Grumman was able to check the electromagnetic compatibility of the Tomcat avionics suite, ensuring that the individual items did not interfere with one another. Maintenance and re-liability demonstration work was carried out using

OPPOSITE TOP
Test flying resumed on 24 May 1971 with the first flight of the second prototype, buno 157981. An A-6 Intruder is flying chase
(Grumman via Robert F Dorr)

ABOVE
*Prototypes 2, 4, and 1X demonstrate the forward, mid-
sweep and full-aft position of the Tomcat's variable sweep
wing*
(Grumman)

OPPOSITE TOP
*Aircraft No 3, buno 157982, seen here carrying only a
light load of AIM-7 Sparrows, was used to clear the
Tomcat at increasing airspeeds and loadings*
(Grumman)

ABOVE
First aircraft to be delivered by Grumman was the No 4 prototype, buno 157983. This was sent to the US Navy's Pacific Missile Test Center at Point Mugu, California, where it received the first AWG-9 weapon system and Phoenix missiles to fly on an F-14
(Grumman)

OVERLEAF
The fifth prototype, buno 157984, was also assigned to Point Mugu, but was lost in an accident on 20 June 1973. A warheadless AIM-7E-2 missile pitched up moments after being launched, and struck the Tomcat
(R Besecker Collection via Robert F Dorr)

the 14th aircraft, while prototypes 15, 16, 18 and 19 were assigned to pilot training. The 17th aircraft was re-assigned to carrier compatability trials following the loss of No 10. No 20—the final prototype—was used for climatic trials at Point Mugu, and was tested in the weather hangar at that facility.

Early spin investigations involved the hand

Only one F-14B prototype—seen here wired with instrumentation for ground tests—was built. Cancellation of the Pratt & Whitney F401 engine halted the development of this improved Tomcat. A-6 Intruders are visible in the background, and an ex-'Blue Angels' Tiger sits forlornly in left-hand corner (Grumman)

launching of a scale model into the spin tunnel at NASA's Langley Research Center. These gave cause for concern, the model displaying a tendency to enter a fast, flat spin. A follow-on investigation in which 1/10 scale unpowered radio-controlled models were released from helicopters, dived to build up speed, then pulled up into a stall, were much more favourable. Models could only be spun if the operator deliberately held the controls in spin-inducing positions. During model tests in the Langley 30 × 60 ft (9 × 18 m) tunnel, a model successfully maintained a 32 degree angle of attack with no tendency to enter a spin.

Early flight tests revealed minor buffeting when the flaps were lowered. Turbulent air resulting from

the airflow through a gap between the spoilers and wing flaps was impinging on the tail surfaces, causing the problem. This gap only existed when the flaps were retracted, and was eliminated by extending the spoilers further aft. Another minor aerodynamic problem noted on early test flights was the generation at high angles of attack of a vortex by the upper corner of the air intake.

A more serious problem was that of engine stalls under some high angle of attack conditions. These were first noted at high angles of attack, when flying at high-altitudes and low speeds. Engines stalled when coming out of afterburner, and at low power settings. On one occasion, a TF30 stalled completely, and the resulting overtemperature wrecked the engine.

Tomcat flights are carried out in a corridor of the Atlantic coastal air-defence identification zone. Located off Long Island, this test area is around 100 miles (160 km) in length. The position of Grumman aircraft within this area is monitored using an IFF tracking station.

Three KA-6 tanker aircraft—originally A-6 development aircraft Nos 3, 4 and 7—were fitted with 'buddy pack' flight-refuelling systems and used to support F-14 operations. Each carried 20,000 lb (9000 kg) of fuel which could be transferred to an F-

14 trials aircraft at a rate of more than 200 gallons per minute (900 litres/min). In-flight refuelling of a Tomcat normally took around ten minutes. With pilot fatigue the main limiting factor, Grumman were able to clock up long test flights. By the end of 1971, test flights involving up to six in-flight refuellings had been recorded.

Traditional methods of flight testing often resulted in length delays in data processing. Analysis of data from a single mission could take up to 14 days, so aircraft would often have flown again before test results became available. To ease the task of flight test, Grumman developed an automated telemetry system able to handle the flow of data from aircraft on test. This is able to handle data from up to three aircraft at once, analyzing selected data in real time (i.e. as fast as it is generated by the aircraft).

ATS was not specifically installed for the F-14 programme. Ordered in 1968, it was first used on the A-6 programme. This proved so successful that the company was able to sell a similar system to NASA's Flight Test Center at Edwards AFB, California, for use with the flight tests of the original prototypes of the Rockwell International B-1 bomber. Having invested heavily in ATS, Grumman uses it for all experimental and development flight testing. In

BELOW
Test flight of the sole F-14B, buno 157986, seventh of the original series of prototype Tomcats
(Grumman)

OVERLEAF
By using KA-6 Intruder tanker aircraft, Grumman was able to extend the duration of test sorties, greatly speeding development of the Tomcat
(Grumman)

winter of 1984–85, telemetry from the X-29 forward-swept wing demonstrator was transmitted to Calverton via a communications satellite.

Using the ATS system, engineers were able to sit at ground-based consoles, monitoring the progress of each test flight. Depending on the type of mission being flown, data could be displayed within five minutes or even in real time. Hard copies of the data appearing on the ground-based CRTs could be obtained at the touch of a button. Another useful ATS function was the ability to set 'redline' limits on all telemetry parameters. Limits could take the form of high or low limits, or even rate-of-change values.

LEFT
The second prototype 'tops up' from the tanker's drogue. Tomcat has a neat retractable probe, whose tip may easily be seen from the cockpit
(Grumman)

BOTTOM LEFT
As this demonstration flight by the second prototype proves, Tomcat is stable at high angles of attack. Pilots converting from the F-4 to the F-14 discover a new freedom to indulge in air combat manoeuvres, but they must still bear in mind the limitations of the TF30 turbofan
(Grumman)

BELOW
These temporary canards were fitted to the No 2 prototype prior to spinning trials
(Grumman)

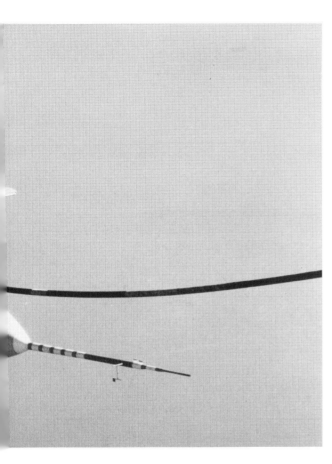

Any parameters exceeding the pre-defined limits was immediately displayed on the console CRTs.

Data from aircraft-mounted sensors was encoded using pulse-code modulation, a signal drawn from the pilots microphone being superimposed. The resulting signal was then transmitted to the ground via an L-band (1.437–1.472GHz) radio link using antennas located at the top of one vertical fin and on the lower fuselage. This telemetry was received by an antenna located at Terry Hill, some 3.5 miles (5.6 km) from the telemetry facility at Calverton's Plant 7. Three Control Data Corporation (CDC) 1700 processors—each able to handle the data from a single F-14—calibrated the incoming information and carried out 'redline' checks before passing the information to the main CDC 6400 computer. By the time that the pilot had completed his post-flight debriefing, all ground-based data processing was completed.

Long sorties and the use of ATS allowed Grumman and the USN to cut around 18 months from the development cycle of the F-14, deploying the aircraft with the fleet in the first half of 1974. Experience gained on earlier programmes allowed Grumman and the USN to integrate activities such as flight test, carrier compatibility trials, air and ground crew training, and the formation of the first operational squadrons into a single unified programme.

Preliminary evaluation of the aircraft by the service was carried out under a three-phase programme. The first Naval Preliminary Evaluation (NPE) carried out in late 1971 studied the aircraft's flying qualities, maintainability and availability, and suitability for use from carriers. Further trials in 1972 continued exploration of the flight envelope and checked out the avionics and weaponry.

Grumman's design and engineering facilities are located at Bethpage, some 35 miles (56 km) northeast of New York, but not all of the Tomcat is built here. Some 60 per cent of F-14 production is handled by more than 150 subcontractors. The entire aft fuselage is supplied by Fairchild Republic's Farmingdale plant, located on Long Island not far from Grumman's Bethpage works, while the same company's Hagerstown plant builds the tail fin and rudder assemblies. Rohr Industries builds the engine inlet ducts and aft nacelles, while Aeronaca tackles the speed brakes and tail-section access doors. Kaman Aerospace is responsible for the wing surfaces, leading edge devices, slats, flaps and spoilers, Sargent Industries provides the titanium wing pivot bearings, while Hamilton Standard produces the wing-sweep actuator.

The main landing gear strut, main landing gear trace, and nose landing gear strut are all built by

Initial catapult trials took place from the Naval Air Test Center at Pax River, Maryland (Grumman)

The 'cat and bomb' logo may date back to the days of biplanes, but the 'Tomcatters' of VF-31 now fly the US Navy's biggest and best fighter. A technician checks the avionics in the rear cockpit (Grumman)

Bendix, while B F Goodrich supplies the wheels, tyres, and brakes. Goodyear Aerospace provides the carbon brakes. Martin-Baker in England has traditionally been the favoured supplier of ejection seats for the US Navy. Tomcat is fitted with the company's GRU-7A seat. Canopies and windshields are provided by Swedlow, the nose radome by Brunswick.

Garrett AiResearch plays a major role under the aircraft's skin, being responsible for the environmental control refrigeration system, temperature control system, central air data computing system, air inlet control system, cabin pressure system, and ATS200-500 engine starter. Gull Airborne Instruments provides the fuel quantity measuring system, engine instruments, flap indicator, and AOA indicator. The emergency generator system and integrated drive generator are

delivered by Sundstrand Aviation. Actuators are supplied by Bendix (horizontal stabilizer servo cylinder and rudder servo actuator), Marquardt (inlet control servo cylinder), Pleaseu Dynamics (ram air door actuators), and the National Water Lift Division of Pneumo (spoiler and pitch servos, also flight control components).

The aircraft is divided into seven main sections, all of which are built, then delivered ready fitted with all electronics and other sub-systems. Grumman's Bethpage works builds the forward and mid-fuselage section, including the vital wing box which forms the structural heart of this part of the aircraft.

The company invested about $3.0 million in electron-beam welding facilities in the late 1960s, installing three Sciaky machines, (one of which was purchased from Boeing following the abandonment of their SST programme). Electron guns in these chambers can operate at voltages of up to 60 kV, and current of up to 500 mA, allowing welding speeds of 100 inch/sec or more. Before welding begins, the EBW chamber is pumped out to a high vacuum—a process which takes less than 20 minutes. This ensures that the welded joints are not contaminated by atmospheric gases, which could cause cracking.

More than 30 parts are electron-welded together to create the completed wing box. No seams are visible on the finished component—to the naked eye, this complex part looks like single mass of intricately-shaped titanium. The resulting structure is tough—after the crash of the short-lived first prototype, the wing box was recovered in excellent condition, and pressed into service as a master component. Although hardly the sort of advertisement the company would have wished, it illustrated the mechanical strength of this critical component. Despite the high technology involved in its construction, the wing box is not expensive to fabricate. Even at the early stages of production, it was the second-least expensive item (in terms of dollars per pound) on the aircraft.

Once the forward fuselage has been assembled, it is mated with the engine nacelles, inlets, and wing gloves. Once completed, the entire Bethpage-assembled forward section of the aircraft is trucked 45 miles (72 km) further up Long Island to Grumman's Calverton facility for final assembly and flight test. More remote from the built-up Bethpage area and from Kennedy International Airport, it is a better location for the inherently noisy task of flight-testing a supersonic fighter.

Into the Calverton works flow Tomcat modules from the various suppliers, plus the Bethpage-built forward fuselages. All these components finally come together at Plant 6. Aircraft factories can often resemble 'dark satanic mills', but Plant 6 presents a scrupulously clean appearance which would put most of its rivals to shame. Management divides the plant into two areas, which compete for cleanliness. The 'FOD Squads' which carry out the regular inspections of each area are made up not of management, but from personnel from the rival area.

The result is a near spotless production line which gives the visitor the distinct impression that any random spot on the floor could be used as a make-shift operating table for an emergency appendectomy with little fear of post-operative infection.

Individual subassemblies are mated at Calverton to create the recognizable beginnings of a Tomcat. At station 1 on the line, the undercarriage is fitted, fuel cells are installed, and the final hydraulic systems are fitted, along with cockpit instrumentation. Station 2 is responsible for tasks such as installing the wing, mating the pivots of the latter with the wing box. In order to cope with the oversweep position used when parking the aircraft, the wing pivots (and the telescoping fuel lines used to link the wing-mounted integral tanks with the main fuel system) incorporate a degree of vertical freedom. At station 3 checks are carried out on the hydraulics, including the wing sweep mechanism. The entire assembly process takes between 65 and 70 days per aircraft. Normal finish of Tomcat—gray polyurathane gloss—is then applied in the Calverton paint shop. Each aircraft must fire 500 rounds from its 20 mm cannon before delivery. To meet this contractual requirement, each Tomcat is moved to Calverton's gun butts, and set up to fire its test rounds up at short range into a target backed with sand.

The newly-built aircraft requires an average of three flights before being accepted by the Navy. Aircraft pass through a 'fly-fix-fly' cycle until all the defects are fixed. Target for the Grumman test team is, of course, to produce a faultless aircraft. In the early stages of the programme such 'zero-defect' aircraft were uncommon, but as experience built up, an increasing number of aircraft were accepted by the US Navy after only a single test flight. After accepting the aircraft from Grumman, the service normally fly around two sorties from Calverton.

Chapter 2
Weapons and sensors

Any combat aircraft is only as good as its armament. To provide the 'teeth' for Tomcat, the US Navy turned to Hughes Aircraft. Brainchild of the legendary Howard Hughes, this is the only US aerospace company to be a market leader in the fields of fighter radar and air-to-air missiles. Rival radar manufacturer Westinghouse does not build missiles, while Raytheon and Ford Aerospace—the other US suppliers of air-to-air missles—cannot match Hughes' fighter radar expertize.

The Hughes AWG-9 pulse Doppler radar was originally developed in the 1960s along with the AIM-54 Phoenix missile as the armament of the ill-fated F-111B interceptor. The design was based on that of an even earlier set, the ASG-1B developed by Hughes first for the F-108 Rapier Mach 3 fighter, then for the experimental YF-12 fighter version of the Lockheed SR-71 Blackbird. The former was cancelled at an early stage of development, the latter never entered production. The massive GAR-9 missile of both aircraft is often considered as an ancestor of the AIM-54 Phoenix, but this is an oversimplistic view. GAR-9 was an infrared homing weapon.

After the cancellation of the F-111B, the AWG-9 design was updated for use on the F-14. This involved reconfiguring the hardware for use in a tandem-seat rather than a side-by-side cockpit, adding the ability to fire shorter range weapons such as Sparrow, Sidewinder and the 20 mm cannon, and displaying the firing envelopes of these weapons on the pilot's head-up display. Despite these additions, the power output of the set was increased, while the weight of the system was cut from around 1,760 lb (800 kg) down to 1,235 lb (560 kg), while the space needed fell from 0.87 cubic metres to 0.78.

The set incorporates a lightweight 5400B digital computer whose maximum processing speed of 550,000 operations per second eclipses that of the AP101 computer carried by the NASA's Space Shuttle, and faster than the AP-1 and 362F computers of the F-15 and F-16. This 24bit device has a thin-film memory used to store tactical software, and core memory which serves as a scratch pad to store intermediate results of computations, for programme storage, and to handle input/output functions.

Despite its age, AWG-9 still has the longest range of any known air-interception set—more than 110 nm (210 km). A fighter-sized target of around five square metres radar cross-section may be detected across a 135 nm (250 km) wide front and two and a half times the range possible with the AWG-10 radar of the F-4J Phantom. AWG-9 also has the ability to carry out near-simultaneous long-range missile launches against up to six targets while tracking 24 more. This capability is not matched by any other interceptor in the east or west, but it does not come cheap—estimated unit cost of the system is around $2.2 million.

OPPOSITE TOP
Like the F-4 Phantom which it replaced, Tomcat was originally planned as a multi-role fighter. This early publicity shot includes not only (front to rear) AIM-9 Sidewinder missiles, 20 mm cannon ammunition, AIM-7 Sparrow missiles, and AIM-54A Phoenix missiles, but also air-to-ground munitions including retarded bombs. In USN service the Tomcat is used as an interceptor and, more recently, as a reconnaissance aircraft—the type has never carried 'mud-moving' ordnance (Grumman)

OPPOSITE BOTTOM
A technician prepares to remove one of the line-replaceable units (LRUs) of the AWG-9 weapon system. The double row of tiny dipole atennas on the main flat-plate antenna are used by the IFF system. The slim fairing under the nose houses antennas for the ALQ-100 jamming system (Grumman)

The antenna is a 36 inch (91.4 cm) diameter flat-plate unit, a type less susceptible to some types of jamming than a traditional parboloidal 'dish' of similar size. The IFF antennas are mounted directly on the antenna, and take the form of an array of dipoles. Output power is 10.2 kW, almost double the 5.2 kW of the APG-63 radar carried by the F-15A, and more than 20 times the power of the APG-59 fitted to early Phantoms. This gives the set a good ability to operate in the face of hostile ECM, burning through jamming signals in order to detect and track its targets.

In normal operation, a radar must transmit at a low enough PRF to allow each pulse sufficient time to make the round trip out to the target and back before the next is transmitted. For a target at a range of 80 nm (150 km), the PRF must be 1 kHz or less, with the radar waiting for up to 1 millisecond between pulses. Pulse-Doppler radars must encode the pulses of a high-PRF Doppler waveform so that range information can be extracted by means of signal processing techniques. In the AWG-9, a modulation is applied to a portion of each pulse, and range is

The principal displays needed by the pilot are located in a vertical 'stack' directly in front of the seat and control column. The large rectangular screen is the Vertical Display Indicator, while the Horizontal Situation Display is located just in front of the control column. The rectangular panel at the top of the instrument panel is for weapons control, while the head-up display is located immediately above
(Grumman)

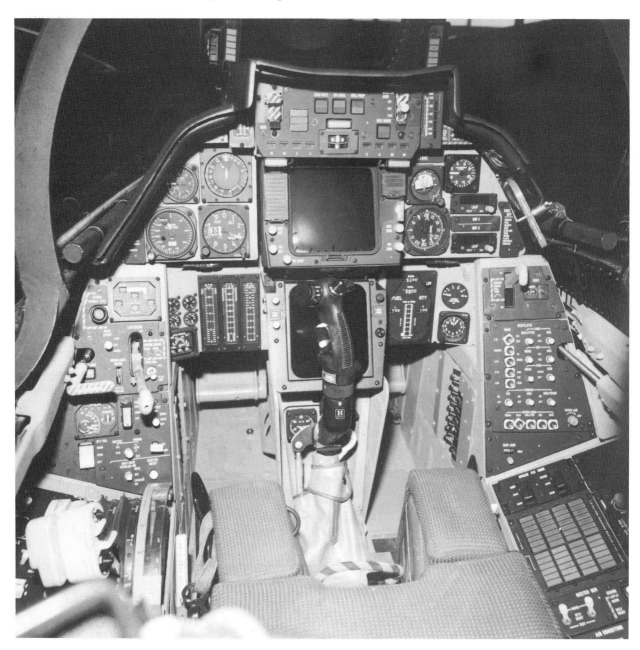

calculated by noting the frequency difference between the modulated and unmodulated portions of the returned pulse.

When operating in pulse-Doppler mode, the set can detect targets out the maximum which the sensitivity of the receiver will allow while using a 250 kHz PRF. Average power on target is therefore 250 times that of a conventional pulse radar. Range data obtained in this way is less accurate than that derived directly from a low-PRF waveform, but is accurate enough for the tracking of long-range targets.

In Pulse-Doppler Search (PDS) mode, the AWG-9 can be used for long-range search, locating five square metre targets at ranges of 200 km or more, and distinguishing them by velocity differences in the returned signal. AWG-9 can look down into ground or sea clutter, detecting and tracking small targets flying at low level. The effects of clutter are removed by a signal processor which uses analogue filtering based on a bank of crystal filters. The set can scan through plus or minus 10, 20, 40 or 65 degrees of azimuth, carrying out one, two, four, or eight-bar elevation searches.

Track-While-Scan (TWS) is used for multiple-target tracking and multi-shot Phoenix engagements.

The rear cockpit is dominated by the circular Tactical Information Display (TID), and by the Hand Control Unit. Most of the major controls for the AWG-9 are located on the large panel above the TID (Grumman)

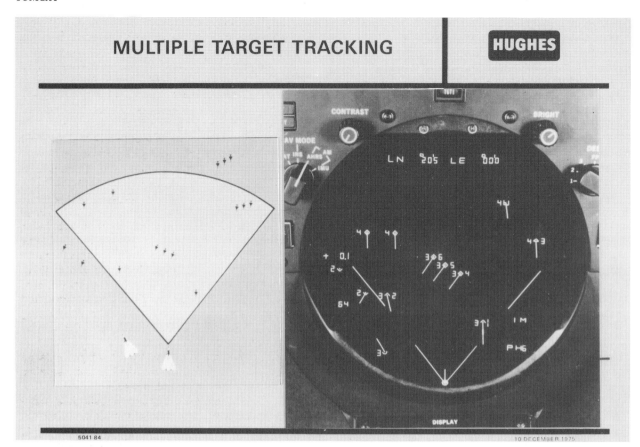

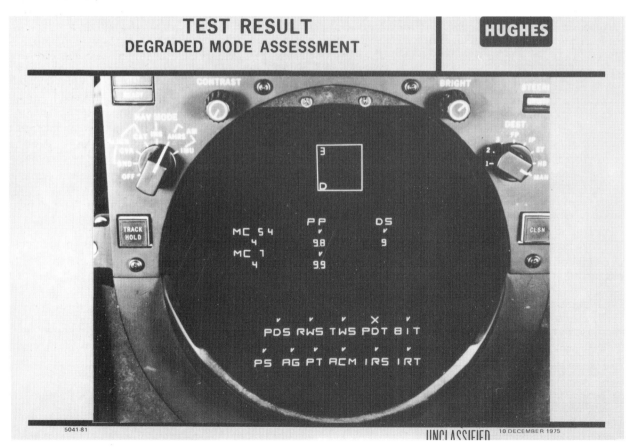

The antenna can perform a plus or minus 40 degree two-bar scan, or a four-bar scan with plus or minus 20 degrees of azimuth cover. As each target within the volume of sky under surveillance is detected, the AWG-9 determines the range and angular position, then passes the information to the central computer where it can be compared with the predicted positions of targets already detected. If the newly-detected target can be correlated with an existing track file, then the latter is updated to show current position. If it cannot, a new track file is established for what is assumed to be a fresh target. Using data such as range, closing velocity, and flight path direction, the computer assigns threat priorities to each track, marking the six highest-priority threats with numerical symbols 1–6 on the display. This mode is also used for multi-shot Phoenix engagements against up to six targets. Maximum missile range in this mode is 90 km. In Range-While-Search (RWS) mode, the set provides range and angular data without stopping the normal antenna TWS search pattern.

If an attack is to made with a single Phoenix missile, Pulse-Doppler Single-Target Track (PDSTT) mode is selected. This locks the AWG-9 antenna on to a single long-range target at ranges of up to 70 nm (130 km), giving range, range-rate and angular data. The missile can be launched at 54 nm (100 km) range. A Jam Angle Track (JAT) facility in this mode may be used to provide range-rate and angular information on targets protected by powerful ECM. A final pulse-Doppler mode allows the radar to be slaved to the aircraft's electro-optical sighting unit in order to obtain range, range-rate and angular data on the target being observed by this passive equipment. In addition to these pulse-Doppler modes, the AWG-9 also has conventional pulse modes for use at short and medium ranges.

Despite the complexity of the AWG-9, reliability is good. In redesigning the equipment for use in the F-14, Hughes was able to improve the design and to use more modern technology. All semiconductor components used in the set are tested before use. The AWG-9's built-in test facilities allow faults to be diagnosed down to LRU level.

AWG-9 and the Phoenix missile were tested both on the ground and in the air against all known types of jamming, Hughes reported, but their optimism was not matched by the British MoD, which told Parliament in 1976 that the AWG-9/Phoenix was considered too vulnerable to jamming.

A modification programme begun in the early 1980s expands the memory of the AWG-9 computer from 32K to 64K memory locations. The expanded memory will consist of four AN/AYK-14(V) memory modules, and reduces the weight, volume and cooling needed by the computer system. Existing sets are being modified under a retrofit programme. Since the current standard of tactical software used by the computer is compatible with the normal or expanded memory, it may be used in any Tomcat.

As part of an upgrading programme associated with the planned introduction of the improved AIM-54C Phoenix missile, the AWG-9 was to have been fitted with a programable digital signal processor. Known as the Target Identification Device/Programmable Signal Processor (TID/PSP), this would have facilitated beyond-visual-range attacks, reducing the need for pre-launch visual identification of targets. Information in the radar return signal not currently exploited by the radar (such as Doppler returns from the different engine types and skin shape) would have allowed positive identification of targets. Under the planned programme, Hughes would have flight-tested a modified AWG-9 system, then delivered it with the first 23 systems in Fiscal Year 1983 but the scheme was adandoned.

The rear cockpit contains two displays—a large circular Tactical Information Display and a smaller rectangular Detailed Data Display.

The Hughes AIM-54 Phoenix missile is a long-range weapon powered by a solid-propellent rocket motor. It operates in conjunction with the AWG-9, and relies on a combination of semi-active radar (SAR) mid-course guidance, plus active-radar terminal homing. Phoenix is intended to engage multiple aircraft or missile targets at long range, destroying them with a conventional warhead even in the face of heavy jamming. Each Tomcat may carry up to six rounds. The programme began back in 1960, when the basic concept was outlined and a competition begun. Hughes was selected in August 1962 to develop the missile, and flight trials started in 1965. Initial tests used unguided rounds, but fully guided XAIM-54 flights started in the following year from two A-3 Skywarrior testbeds and a single F-111B aircraft. The first guided shot scored a hit at a range twice that of the best air-to-air missiles of the time.

Test missiles were procured in Fiscal Years 1968 and 1969, and a production contract for the AIM-54A was awarded to Hughes in December 1970. Testing of this version ended in FY72. Production of the AIM-54A was concluded in 1981 after Hughes had manufactured more than 2,500 at its Tucson, Arizona, manufacturing plant.

Fuselage and aerodynamic surfaces of Phoenix are all made from metal, but the fuselage is covered with

OPPOSITE PAGE
Tactical Information Display (TID) symbology displayed on the RIO's rear-cockpit console (Hughes)

OVERLEAF
This aircraft from VF-213 'Black Lions' carries all three current air-to-air missiles. These are (from left to right) AIM-9 Sidewinder, AIM-7 Sparrow and AIM-54 Phoenix

ablative thermal insulation. Directly behind the nose radome is the planar array seeker antenna, followed by the transmitter/receiver and the electronics unit. Next comes the fuzing and arming system, the former consisting of contact and proximity fuzes. The warhead is a 132 lb (60 kg) high-explosive charge. Based on the continuous-rod principle, it can create massive damage to aircraft structures.

The aft section of the missile (around half the fuselage length) contains the powerplant, a single stage Rocketdyne MK47 solid-propellant motor. This steel-cased unit has a long burn time, and the power needed to blast the round to speeds of up to Mach 5 at high altitudes, although speeds are much slower at lower levels.

Like previous Hughes air-to-air missiles such as the Falcon series, Phoenix is steered by tail-mounted control surfaces. According to Hughes, this scheme offers lower drag and higher manoeuvrability than the moving wings used by weapons such as Sparrow. On trials, Phoenix has manoeuvered at 17G. Hydraulic actuators and an associated power system are packed into the rear of the missile. Along with the

electrical conversion unit and power supply, they are wrapped around the motor tailpipe.

The missile's powerful motor, long flight time and wide antenna gimbal angle make the interceptor's task easy. Launch Acceptability Regions (LARs) are large compared with those of shorter range weapons. When Japan evaluated the F-14, it was informed that the maximum launch range of Phoenix was typically five times that of the Japan Air Self Defense Force's principle air-to-air missile.

After launch, the weapon can use three types of guidance. For long-range shots, during the first stages of flight, the missile flies a pre-programmed course under autopilot control. In mid-course flight, the nose-mounted seeker takes over, operating in semi-active mode. If the launch aircraft's AWG-9 radar is set for Track-While-Scan operation, the target is not continually illuminated, so the Phoenix

ABOVE
Test firing of AIM-54A from a Phoenix Missile System trials aircraft based at Point Mugu
(Hughes Aircraft)

BELOW
An AIM-54 round—already clipped to its launch rail—in position under the belly of a Tomcat and ready to be lifted into position
(Jean-Pierre Montbazet)

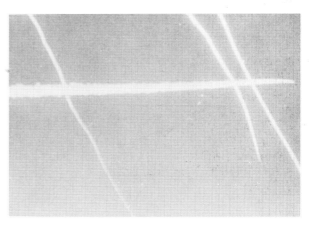

Final proof of Phoenix's effectiveness—a single Tomcat engages six targets with six missiles on 22 November 1973. All the rounds were fired in a period of 38 seconds from a Tomcat flying at Mach 0.78/28,400 ft (5600 m) over Point Mugu at drone targets between 31 and 50 nm (57–92 km) away. Target speeds varied from Mach 0.6 to 1.1 at altitudes between 22,00–24,000 ft (6700–7300 m). One missile failed when a fault developed in its antenna control loop, while another had the misfortune to be released against a drone which later veered off course and failed to provide a realistic radar target. The remaining four scored direct hits. The final photo in the sequence shows the contrail of the final missile crossing those of earlier rounds in the same salvo (Hughes Aircraft)

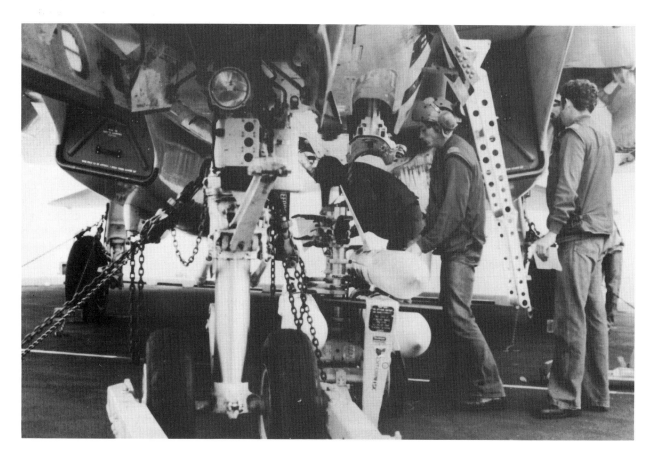

This F-14, buno 158615, was photographed in the inventory of the trials fleet at the Pacific Missile Test Center (PMTC) at Point Mugu on 20 May 1977 (R Besecker Collection via Robert F Dorr)

Armourers trundle AIM-7 Sparrow missiles into position using a loading trolley. Note the lowered position of one of the rams used to force the round clear of the fuselage at the moment of launch (Grumman)

guidance system receives only samples of radar data.

Long missile range demands that demands on missile energy (i.e. velocity) be minimized. On maximum-range missions, Phoenix does not fly directly towards the target but is lofted into a high trajectory designed to reduce interference between the AWG-9's powerful transmitter and the missile-borne receiving system, and to minimize aero-dynamic drag. Induced drag results from missile manoeuvres, and is minimized by the missile's aft-mounted control surfaces. On a maximum-range mission, the round can have a flight time of up to three minutes.

When switched to active-radar mode the missile seeker has a maximum range of 9–11 nm (16 to 20 km). Once this has been done, the missile is independent of its parent aircraft and will continue to home without outside assistance. If fired from the aircraft at 11 nm (20 km) or less, the round will automatically carry out an immediate target-aquisition, flying all the way to impact as an active-radar 'fire-and-forget' weapon.

Some sources have suggested the existence of a 'flyout' mode which would allow the missile to tackle stand-off jammers on which the AWG-9 cannot obtain lock. This presumes that the missile could fly most of the way to the target under autopilot control, switching to its built-in seeker in the final stages of flight.

Phoenix rounds have been fired against many types of target. A crucial test was carried on in November 1973, when a single Tomcat fired six Phoenix rounds in the space of 38 seconds against targets between 27 and 43 nm (50–80 km) away. One missile went off course, another had no target to engage (the offending drone developed a fault while the Phoenix was in flight), but the other four made successful interceptions.

Other trials pitted Phoenix against simulations of the best aircraft which the Soviet Air Force possessed in the 1970s. Tests against simulated MiG-25 *Foxbat* targets—Bomarc missiles flying at speeds of Mach 2.7 at more than 80,000 ft (24,400 m) and fitted with an augmentation system which made its radar echoing area resemble that of *Foxbat*—have left no doubt that the weapon would be effective against the Soviet Mach 3 fighter. To simulate a Tupolev Tu-22M *Backfire*, a drone was flown at Mach 1.5 at 50,000 ft (15,250 m), and fitted with a noise jammer. A Phoenix released from a Tomcat flying at Mach 1.5 at 44,000 ft (13,400 m) flew for 110 nm (203 km) and made a perfect interception. During this firing, the missile's energy-management trajectory took the round to a record height of 103,500 ft (31,550 m) during the mid-course stages of flight.

Other tests matched Phoenix against difficult targets intended to prove the weapon's capability. A BQM-34 drone was flown at a height of only 50 ft (15 m) above the sea to simulate a Soviet anti-ship cruise missile, then engaged by a Tomcat flying 22 nm (41 km) away at Mach 0.72 at 10,000 ft (3000 m). Sixteen seconds after a Phoenix had been launched against it from a Tomcat cruising at Mach 0.7 and 10,000 ft (3000 m), a QF-86 drone version of the F-86 Sabre was put through a series of manoeuvres intended to attempt to break the lock of the AWG-9 radar. From its Mach 0.8 flight at 15,300 ft (4660 m), the target entered a 5G manoeuvre, then into a vertical dive, before pulling a 6G manoeuvre and resuming horizontal flight at 9,100 ft (2770 m). Phoenix made a successful interception just as the target pulled out of its dive.

Another trial tested missile performance against an attacker screened by an escorting jamming aircraft. The aircraft—a drone version of an obsolete Grumman F9 fighter flew at Mach 0.8 and 36,000 ft (11,000 m) while a jammer-equipped BQM-34A followed 25 nm (46 km) behind and at the same speed

The AIM-9 Sidewinder is tolerant of odd carriage angles, so may be fitted on the side of an underwing pylon (US Navy via Robert F Dorr)

OPPOSITE TOP
Close-up of the chin-mounted sensors. The cylindrical fairing contains the optics of the Northrop AXX-1 Television Camera Sight, while the smaller housing below it contains antennas for the ALQ-100 jamming system. The muzzle of the 20 mm cannon is located on the port side of the fuselage, and the muzzle-end of the clustered six barrels may be seen at the far right (Grumman)

OPPOSITE BOTTOM
Before delivery to the US Navy, every Tomcat is taken to the gun butts at Calverton so that its 20 mm cannon may be test-fired (Grumman)

but a higher cruise altitude of 35,500 ft (10,800 m). The first Phoenix was launched against the QF-9 at a range of 25 nm (46 km) while a second released nine seconds later was targetted against the BQM-34A. Both scored kills.

The characteristics of the latest types of Soviet air-launched anti-ship missile complicate the task of USN air-defence interceptors. Longer missile range allows rounds to be fired from greater stand-off distances, making the engagement of the carrier aircraft prior to missile release more difficult. Higher missile speeds coupled with more elusive flight profiles greatly complicate the task of defensive SAMs and probably the AIM-54s.

The Navy is currently in the early stages of buying around 3,460 improved AIM-54C missiles in a programme likely to run beyond the year 1990 at a cost of approximately $4.1 billion. This modified weapon is intended to cope with the upgraded Soviet threat, but the move to field an improved Phoenix was at least partly spurred by the knowledge that the AIM-54A may have been compromised in the late 1970s in the political chaos which followed the Iranian revolution. Modifications were hastily made

to USN AIM-54A rounds following the Iranian Revolution to minimize the usefulness of any Phoenix data which Soviet agents might have been able to obtain.

Engineering development of the AIM-54C started in October 1976, and Hughes delivered the first engineering development models in August 1979. This was completed in December 1980 with the delivery of 15 such models to the US Navy. Firing trials went well, with the first three rounds launched all passing with lethal distance of drone targets. Pilot production of 30 rounds for evaluation started in October 1981, and the first production standard AIM-54Cs left the line on schedule late in 1983,

under a $44 million contract from Naval Air Systems Command. The decision to go to full production was taken in January of the following year.

The difference between the old and new versions of Phoenix are largely confined to the guidance system, and include a solid-state transmitter/receiver assembly for the seeker head, a programmable digital signal processor, and a new digital autopilot, strapdown inertial reference unit, and fuzing system. The new digital systems replace older analogue circuitry, allowing the missiles to be pre-programmed by software to allow software programming for stream raid discrimination, improved beam attack and improved rear quarter opening rate capabilities.

The AIM-54C has the ability to take on targets at greater range or higher altitudes, and can cope with higher degrees of target manoeuvrability. Target discrimination has been improved by the installation of the new transmitter/receiver, while the new fuze gives a greater number of target 'kills'—the Motorola DSU-28C/B target detecting device is used to detonate the warhead at the moment in time which maximizes its destructive effect against the target.

Electronic counter-countermeasures (ECCM) facilities have also been upgraded, allowing the AIM-54C to cope with small, very low altitude targets, discriminating between the true target and any chaff released in an attempt to break lock-on. These improvements make Phoenix less vulnerable to the ECM threat posed by the newer Soviet bombers and air-to-surface missiles, says the US DoD. Reference to ASMs suggests that these weapons may carry internal ECM suites intended to counter defensive SAM's and air-to-air missiles.

Production plans for the new missiles called for a total of 3,467 to be built at a production rate rising from an initial 20 per month to an eventual peak of 60 per month. Full production was due to begin by Fiscal Year 1984, but in the summer of 1984 US Navy technicians found signs of poor workmanship in a Phoenix AIM-54C missile shipped in June from Hughes' Tucson plant. On 22 July, the service announced its decision to suspend acceptance of the weapon, until quality problems have been resolved.

In raising its complaints on quality control, the USN made it clear that the weapon has experienced 'no performance or reliability problems', but demanded that improvements be made to soldering, wiring and cleanliness. The problem was probably due at least in part to the sheer success of the company's missiles—in an 18 month period no fewer than five designs had been committed to production, forcing an expansion of the workforce. The task of training new manufacturing personnel at a time when the company was very much on a learning curve as the AIM-54C production rate built up, seems to have resulted in the slower-than-desired build-up in production skills, with the newly assembled weapons containing a higher than anticipated number of 'fixes'—instances where parts or assemblies had been

reworked to correct manufacturing defects. The disturbance to deliveries was short-lived. On 23 November the USN resumed progress payments to Hughes, saying that the company had co-operated in correcting the quality-control deficiencies.

The USN also announced in the summer of 1984 that it wanted a second manufacturing source for the missile, but stressed that this was in no way linked to the quality-control problem. The decision to develop a second source had in fact been taken by the Secretary of the Navy on 15 May. Following competitive evaluation of potential second-source

In this 1973 test of Tomcat's air combat manoeuvring capability, Grumman pilot Charles Sewell flew one of the prototypes against a slatted F-4J Phantom flown by US Navy test pilot Lt D Walker (Grumman)

manufacturers, the USN plans to run a ten-round qualification programme in Fiscal Year 1987. The second source would receive orders for 50 and 240 rounds in the two years which followed, and would then be free to bid in direct competition against Hughes in FY1990 and beyond.

The original USN operational requirement for the F-14 specified that a payload of up to 14,500 lb (6600 kg) of ordnance plus two AIM-9 Sidewinders should be possible for interdiction and close-support missions. To help provide this air-to-ground capability, a system of pre-loaded weapon rails was devised. By attaching the ordnance to the rail, then fitting the pre-loader rail onto a clean aircraft, weapon-loading time and thus aircraft turnaround time could be greatly reduced. Individual rails could carry either a Phoenix missile launcher or a 30 inch

ABOVE
Tomcat on target—Sewell slides into position behind the F-4J. In combat the result would be an easy Sidewinder shot (Grumman)

An F-14 flies through smoke and debris after blowing apart a QF-86 target drone with an AIM-9L Sidewinder missile (US Navy)

bomb rack. A built-in hoist mechanism within the rail lifted it into place under the wing. A single-point safe/arm device provided simultaneous control of all the ordance on the rail. Tomcat would have been an effective strike aircraft, able to carry ten Mk 82 bombs to a target 850 nm (1600 km) or more away, but it was never deployed with other than air-to-air armament. The task of replacing the F-4 in the ground-attack role fell to the later F/A-18A.

The Soviet Union has accused the US Government of planning to install the Vought ASAT air-launched anti-satellite missile on the Tomcat. According to a *Pravda* article of 28 February 1984 by U Sadov, 'The plans for the creation by 1987 of more

than 100 anti-satellite systems are truly sinister. It is believed that practically any F-15 aircraft can be swiftly turned into an anti-satellite weapon. Recently plans have been discussed for "modification" of Navy F-14 aircraft to give them anti-satellite functions.'

Medium-range armament of the Tomcat is the Raytheon AIM-7 Sparrow, a semi-active radar missile which serves as the long-range weapon of most other US fighters. Development of the Sparrow missile began in the late 1950s, and more than 34,000 of the earlier AIM-7 C, D, and E models were produced. The -7D and -7E were widely used in Vietnam, but with disappointing results. Like many

missiles of the time, Sparrow was designed at a time when the most likely target was a subsonic non-manoeuvring bomber flying at high altitude. If fired against subsonic manoeuvring targets, or against targets below 5,000 ft (1500 m) it was rarely successful. In 1967, the 366th Tactical Fighter Wing fired 21 Sparrows at North Vietnamese MiGs flying at altitudes below 8,000 ft (2400 m), but they all missed.

A redesigned effort resulted in the more manoeuvrable and reliable AIM-7E-2 and -7E-3, with clipped wings, improved autopilots and better fuzing. The later -7E-4 model was specifically designed to work with high-powered fighter radars such as Tomcat's AWG-9, but the biggest improvement came in 1977 with the introduction of the AIM-7F. Drastically redesigned from nose to tail, this substituted solid-state electronics for the miniature vacuum tube technology of the earlier versions. On the -7E the guidance and seeker occupied the entire front section of the missile forward of the moveable wings. Aft of these surfaces came the warhead, then the rocket motor. In the -7F, miniaturization allowed the warhead to be moved forward of the wings and their associated actuators, and greatly increased in size. The volume aft of the wings could now be almost entirely devoted to the rocket motor.

Early Sparrows had used a short-burning boost motor, and glided unpowered for most of the way to long-range targets, while the AIM-7E used a lower-thrust sustainer motor with a longer burn time. For the AIM-7F, a dual-thrust booster/sustainer was used. Flying under sustainer power, this had a much longer range of up to 28 to 30 miles (45–50 km), about twice that of the -7E. This figure refers to a head-on engagement. In tail-chase interceptions it can fall to only 3 to 5 miles (5–8 km)—for a high-speed target the closing rate between the missile and its victim is much lower. Since the missile has only a limited duration of powered and guided flight, it must be released much closer to the target to effect an interception in the time available.

The new seeker was compatible with modern pulse-Doppler radars, but still retained the conical scanned antenna used in earlier models, a potential Achilles' Heel in the face of modern deception jamming. One feature which significantly increased ECM resistance was the fact that the guidance system was given the range to the target before the missile was fired. Since the seeker could measure target velocity from the Doppler return of the reflected signal, it could continuously update its range data. Knowledge of target speed and range was of great assistance in rejecting chaff or the effects of deception jamming. The earlier -7E had measured target range by comparing a modulated signal transmitted by the launch aircraft (and received via a small rearward-facing antenna) with the same signal as reflected by the target.

Procurement of the AIM-7F was limited to only around 5,000 rounds, while Raytheon developed the AIM-7M. This has an ECM-resistant monopulse seeker with improved look-down capability, and digital signal processing. In all other respects it is similar to the -7F, and most rounds of the latter standard will be rebuilt as AIM-7Ms. The AIM-7M entered production in the early 1980s, and has a unit cost of $203,000—inexpensive by Phoenix standards—but long-term production plans are being reviewed. The USN plans to buy at least 1,000 further rounds in FY85, but the USAF is planning to buy only 4,332 rounds and then switch production to the new Hughes AIM-120A AMRAAM. (Advanced Medium-Range Air-to-Air Missile).

After missile launch, the fighter must continue to illuminate the target. For the F-14, this means staying within a 65 degree cone so that the antenna of the AWG-9 will be able to follow the target. Sparrow has a longer range when fired from the Tomcat than from any other US fighter. Compared with the F-4J, Tomcat can obtain around 40 per cent more range from the missile, thanks to the high transmitter power and high antenna gain of its AWG-9 radar.

For short-range combat, Tomcat relies on the most widely deployed US air-to-air missile, the AIM-9 Sidewinder. This simple heat-seeking missile has been built in large quantities, deliveries having long passed the 180,000 mark. Not all were new missiles, the weapons' modular nature allowed many older patterns to be rebuilt to more modern standards with better seekers and motors, maintaining their effectiveness. The total world inventory of the Sidewinder is believed to be about 80,000 missiles. In the United States, Sidewinder production is shared by Ford Aerospace and Raytheon. Overseas production lines exist in Western Europe and Japan, but the US Government maintains a strict control on the seeker technology used in the AIM-9L version.

The US Navy no longer operates older models such as the AIM-9B, -9C, and -9D. Sizeable stocks still exist of the -9G, and -9H—several thousand of each variant—but the most important models are now the AIM-9L and -9M. Both have seekers able to acquire and lock on to a target from almost any angle; earlier versions could only lock on to the hot tail section of a target aircraft, forcing the Sidewinder-equipped fighter to fly his aircraft into a 'tail-chase' manoeuvre. The -9L and -9M therefore allow much greater tactical freedom in air combat. Used in action during the 1982 Falklands conflict by Royal Navy Sea Harriers and Royal Air Force Harrier GR.3s, AIM-9L was often fired in head-on engagements. It proved highly effective, downing 24 Argentinian aircraft including the Mirage III, IAI Dagger, and A-4 Skyhawk.

The AIM-9L was a joint US Navy/USAF project, and was started in the early 1970s. Production began in 1976 and continued until 1981, when it was replaced by the AIM-9M, currently the only version being supplied to the US services. The only other current production model is the AIM-9P, a version developed exclusively for export. The US Navy is a large-scale purchaser of Sidewinder, ordering an average of 350 to 500 per annum. A modification programme is converting the service's surviving AIM-9H and -9J rounds to -9M standard.

The AIM-9M has a closed-cycle cooling system for the seeker's IR detector, a reduced-smoke rocket motor, plus other modifications. Development started in early 1976, and was completed just over three years later. Successful Initial Operational Test and Evaluation (IOT&E) trials confirmed the missile's superiority to the AIM-9L in target tracking and resistance to background radiation and ECM.

Tomcat was due to carry the AIM-95 Agile, a heat-seeking wingless missile steered by a thrust-vectoring control system. Intended to replace the AIM-9L, it was developed between 1971 and 1975 by the Naval Weapons Center, but like the USAF's AIM-82A 'dogfight' missile, it was abandoned while still under development.

Given the often poor performance of US missiles during the Vietnam war, the reader may well wonder just how effective Tomcat's armament would be in combat. One thing is clear: the era of near 100 per cent combat kills is far distant. Back around 1980, the US Navy estimated the single-shot kill probability of Sidewinder as 0.5, and that of Sparrow as 0.35. The USAF was not so optimistic, claiming only 0.28 for both types, a prediction which probably reflects the smaller and more agile targets which the Air Force would expect to meet in combat. Both figures are well above the kill rates registered during the Vietnam war. In Southeast Asia, only 18 per cent of the Sidewinders fired in anger hit their targets, while the success rate for Sparrow was a mere 9 per cent.

The best evidence available suggests that US air-to-air missiles would score a single-shot kill rate of between 10 and 20 per cent against low-level targets, and anything from 20 to 50 per cent at high altitude. They would probably have similar success rates against fighter targets, but if fired at long range against bombers cruising at medium altitude could down up to 70 per cent of the attackers. Phoenix also has an anti-missile capability. In this role SSKP has been estimated at 15 per cent against weapons flying at medium altitudes, falling to only 5 per cent for low-flying targets.

A single 20 mm General Electric Vulcan M61A1 rotary cannon is carried in the port side of the forward fuselage. This weapon is 74 inches (188 cm) long and weighs approximately 265 lb (120 kg). A muzzle gas diffuser is fitted to avoid structural damage, while a muzzle clamp reduces the dispersal of the rounds fired from its six barrels. A total of 675 rounds are carried in the ammunition drum. To avoid the possibility to spent cases being sucked into the inlet and damaging the engines, the empty cases are returned to the drum after being removed from the gun breech.

The pilot selects and prepares the weapon to be fired. The actual firing can be done by the pilot, the back-seater, or the aircraft's computer. Using his HUD, the pilot can lock the radar on to short-range targets, (10 nm or less) but all long-range targets are handled by the RIO. A TID Repeat mode allows the pilot to view all the computer-generated symbology which the RIO is showing on his TID. The RIO is basically the F-14 systems operator, and is responsible for handling the radar, INS, ECM, communications, and other avionics. The Navy tends to keep pilots and RIOs teamed up as long as possible, In air combat manoeuvring, the pilot is able to concentrate his attention on the target, while the RIO handles ECM systems, launching chaff or flares, and watching for hostile aircraft or missile launches. The EW systems should give warning of an approaching attacker, but in combat involving more than a handful of aircraft, the eyeballs of the RIO are likely to prove more valuable.

In addition to the radar displays, the rear cockpit is fitted with a hand controller used to direct the radar antenna and the seeker head of the chin-mounted TV sensor (if this item is fitted). Also present are the control panels for avionics units such as the TACAN, UHF radio, IFF system, datalink, and the armament control panel used to launch guided missiles.

One item of equipment which was fitted to early-production Tomcats but soon deleted was the chin-mounted ALR-23 infrared search and acquisition set. This was intended to locate targets in the event of the AWG-9 being inoperable, either as a result of malfunction or intense jamming. Its seeker head could be slewed independently of the radar antenna. Its indium-antimonide detectors were cooled by a self-contained Stirling-cycle cryogenic system, while the remainder of the system was cooled by the chilled oil which circulated to the Phoenix missiles.

At the time when Tomcat was in the advanced stages of development and just entering squadron service, the Soviet MiG-25 Foxbat was widely considered to be a major threat. The aircraft's highly-specialized interceptor role was not at that time fully appreciated, the Soviet fighter being often presented as a tri-sonic 'wonder plane'. Grumman was quick to highlight Tomcat's performance in the anti-Foxbat role. Appearing as a relatively hot target against the sky background, Foxbat's airframe and twin Tumansky afterburning turbojet engines would present a near-ideal target to the ALR-23.

In practice, the IR sensor proved ineffective and was deleted, a move which freed the chin position for a much more useful electro-optical aid. The Northrop AXX-1 TCS (Television Camera Sight) is based on the USAF's TISEO equipment. The latter was developed as an offshoot of the USAF's Rivet Haste and Combat Tree programmes of the early 1970s. TISEO consists of a video camera fitted with a stabilized optical telescope and mounted in a fairing on the leading edge of the left wing of some F-4E Phantoms. In conditions of good visibility it allowed

*HUD's eye-view of close combat manoeuvres as one
Tomcat tries to get on the tail of another
(Grumman)*

aircrew to identify another aircraft at ranges well
beyond those possible with the unaided eye.
Although considered for use on the F-15 it was found
to be unsuitable for use in single-seat fighters.

In 1977 the USN began tests of a modified TISEO
known as the TVSU (Television Sight Unit). This
proved successful, allowing aircrew to positively
identify targets and to fire air-to-air missiles before
entering the performance envelope of most Soviet
aircraft/missile combinations. Two to three miles was
typical for aircraft identification with the naked eye,
but TVSU-equipped aircraft could manage nine
miles (14 km) or more. Improvements of 10 to 1 have
been reported, and users can even tell what type of
external stores a target aircraft is carrying.

TVSU went to sea in the summer of 1978 aboard
the carriers *Kennedy* and *Constellation*. 'We flew the
system from early May into August, and did not
perform a single maintenance function during that
time,' reported Cdr Tim Wright, commanding
officer of VF-14. One failure then occurred, but '...
VF-32 never did have a malfunction.' Comments
from *Constellation* were equally enthusiastic. TVSU
was intended for air-to-air use, but crews from VF-24
used their new 'kit' to locate Soviet warships,
identifying these at long range. TVSU project officer

Lt Bryan Rollins reported, 'Let's say there's radar
contact with a ship at 50 miles (80 km). You can lock it
in on radar, slave the TVSU to the radar so you have a
picture of what you're actually looking at on the
radar. At great distances we could see the airplanes
flying the pattern around our carrier.'

By the end of 1987 a total of 398 F-14s will have
been fitted with the definitive TCS (Television
Camera Sight), which is mounted in a fairing under
the nose. Although based on TISEO, it is rugged
enough to withstand carrier use. The X10 optical
system can scan a 30 degree field of view. Wide
(1.42 deg) or narrow (0.44 deg) coverage can be
selected, with black-and-white imagery being presented on the pilot's vertical display indicator and the
RIO's tactical information display. TCS has good
tracking stability under high G loadings, and can be
used to identify targets, to study close formations
which appear as a single large radar target at long
range, and to track targets while the AWG-9 is not
transmitting.

The Central Air Data Computer (CADC) is an
AiResearch CP-1166B/A. Using data from sensors
which measure pilot and static pressures, temperature and angle of attack, this sends commands to the
control surfaces, selects the optimum wing angle, and
passes to the Air Inlet Control Systems (AICS) the
data which the latter needs in order to match the inlet
ramps to airspeed and altitude.

Primary navigation aid of the F-14A is the ASN-
92(V) CAINS II (Carrier Aircraft Inertial Nav-

igation System II). It consists of the ASN-90 Inertial Measurement Unit, Litton LC-728 navigational computer, a control indicator, a convertor amplifier, and a power supply. The system is similar to the basic ASN-92 carried by the A-6E Intruder (in place of the earlier ASN-31) and EA-6B, and being retrofitted into the RF-4B fleet. Prior to take-off, the INS may be linked to the carrier's SINS (Ship's Inertial Navigation System) via Tomcat's microwave data link, and given the details of velocity, heading, and position required for INS alignment, plus up to seven waypoints.

TACAN facilities are provided by the Gould ARN-84. This all solid-state microminiaturized navaid is in widespread use, equipping USAF and US Navy types such as C-130, E-2C, F-5E, F-111F and FB-111A, A-4M, A-7E, S-3A, P-3C, KC-130R, T-38A, AH-1T, CH-53 and SH-3H. Operating at frequencies between 932–1,213 MHz, the ARN-84 provides direct slant range and bearing to any standard TACAN ground beacon or VORTAC ground station.

The AN/ARA-63, the airborne portion of the AACA (Airctaft Approach Control System), uses the AN/SPN-41 and the AN/TRN-28 transmitting sets. It provides either primary or backup instrument approach capability for aircraft. It receives pulse-coded microwave transmissions from the ground or aircraft carrier-based azimuth and elevation transmissions on any of 20 channels. The ARA-63 operates from 15.512 GHz to 14.688 GHz and decodes these signals for display on a crosspoint indicator in the aircraft cockpit. The major components of the ARA-63 are the R-1399 receiver, KY-651 pulse decoder, and the C-7949 receiver control. To complete the airborne subsystem, several types of crosspointer are used. The Multi-Mode Receiver (MMR), unofficially designed as the ARN-128(V)2, is due to replace the ARA-63 in the late 1980s.

Tomcat was originally fitted with the ARC-51A UHF radio, but now uses the ARC-159, the Navy's standard airborne transceiver. This is made of the RT-1150 receiver-transmitter, ID-1972 indicator, C-9451 control, MT-4609 mount, and the SA-1964 switching unit. For secure voice communication, the

BELOW
Test launch of a Phoenix missile from an F-14 of VF-211 'Fighting Checkmates'
(Hughes Aircraft)

OVERLEAF
This F-14A displays the current configuration of the chin fairings—early production Tomcats carried an infrared tracker in the larger of the two housings, but this proved relatively ineffective and was replaced by the Northrop AAX-1
(Northrop)

The AAX-1 television camera set (TCS) allows targets to be identified at long range, allowing missiles to be fired without fear of hitting friendly aircraft (Northrop)

In this test, the AAX-1 provided a clear image of another F-14 at ten times the range possible using 'eyeball' recognition (Northrop)

unit is integrated with the KY-58 cryptographic system. This 9 lb (4 kg) solid-state radio covers the frequency range of 225 to 339.975, has a 10 watt power output, and offers 7,000 channels. Mean Time Between Failure (MTBF) is 1,000 hours. The ARC-192 combined VHF/UHF radio is due to replace the ARC-159, with deployment starting in 1986.

The Harris ASW-27B digital datalink provides high-speed communications between Tomcat and ship-based command and control systems. By means of its digital data link equipment, each F-14 can be linked to the Airborne Tactical Data System (ATDS) of the Fleet's Grumman E-2C Hawkeye early-warning aircraft, and to the Naval Tactical Data System (NTDS) of its parent carrier. Each Tomcat within the combat area has its own unique electronic address code. Within one second, a message may be sent to and received from each F-14 in a squadron.

The link may be used to pass target data, entending the effective radar range of the F-14s and the E-2C.

Data on targets transmitted by the E-2C is stored in the Tomcat's AWG-9 radar and displayed to the aircrew, while data from the fighter (such as current position, altitude and speed) is sent back to the E-2C. By using the datalink, ship-based commanders can allocate target priorities to the F-14. Target data from the AWG-9 may also be transmitted to the E-2C, appearing on the aircraft's radar screens. Thanks to this link, the crew of a Tomcat can have a full 360 degree display of the total combat area. The link is also compatible with the E-3A Sentry AWACS, and the NATO Air Ground Defence Environment.

Like all US warplanes Tomcat carries an array of ECM equipment, including radar-warning receivers, chaff/flare dispensers, and jammers. The US Air Force carries most of its EW equipment in external

A TARPS-equipped Tomcat on test in the Calverton anechoic chamber
(Grumman)

ABOVE
The TARPS AAD-5/RS-720 infrared sensor of the TARPS pod created this IR image of a carrier deck. White = hot, so the white streaks on the deck show the heating effects caused by aircraft running-up their engines. Parked aircraft appear all-black; those showing traces of white have their engines running, or have just shut down. The steam catapults appear as two white stripes at the bottom left
(US Navy)

pods, but the Navy has always favoured internal installations. Pods may be easy to fit, and may be changed if the aircraft must face new threats for which a different pattern of jammer provides better protection, but they occupy a valuable hardpoint and impose a drag penalty. Internal systems avoid such performance losses. Being housed within the aircraft's avionics bays, they tend to be lighter than pods.

Internal fits do have disadvantages however. Constrained by the limited space available within the aircraft, they are often more difficult to change or modify. Pod designers can always add blisters or fairings to their creations in order to house extra equipment, but internal systems must always be crammed into a fixed volume. The long connections needed to link the electronics with their respective antennas introduce loss of signal, but the designer is relatively free to position the antennas on the aircraft in locations which offer good coverage. From some angles, pod mounted systems are often partly screened by the fuselage of the aircraft they are trying to protect, and thus lose effectiveness. Pod antennas are also much closer together than is possible in an internal fit. The electronic isolation between them is

therefore low, with one antenna tending to affect the performance of another.

When the Tomcat first entered service, its radar-warning receivers were the APR-25 and APR-27, units developed during the Vietnam war. The current Magnavox ALR-50 is based on the earlier APR-27. Designed to warn of missile launches, it allows aircrew to activate EW systems or to take evasive manoeuvres. A major update programme modified the equipment in order to deal with the SA-6 *Gainful* missile and its associated *Straight Flush* radar, while other upgrades followed during the 1970s and early 1980s. By the end of the decade, it will have been replaced by the ALR-67.

For the carriage and deployment of chaff, flares and miniature jammers, the aircraft is fitted with the Goodyear ALE-39 dispensing system, which has replaced the ALE-29 originally carried. This operates under manual or automatic control, ejecting

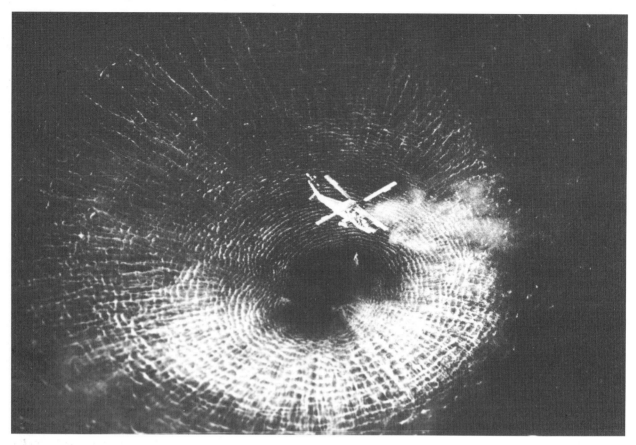

This ghostly negative image of a rescue operation was taken by the KA-99 camera of a TARPS-equipped F-14 of VF-2 'Bounty Hunters'
(US Navy, VF-2)

payloads singly or in pre-programmed combinations, depending on the tactical situation.

Several patterns of internally-mounted jamming equipment have been installed on the Tomcat. The aircraft entered service fitted with the Sanders Associates ALQ-100, a noise deception jammer which covered several frequency bands. Probably developed as an anti-SAM system, it uses track-breaking techniques when operating in deception mode.

The ALQ-100 has now been replaced by the Sanders AN/ALQ-126A, an internally mounted deception jammer carried aboard most US Navy tactical aircraft. Part of the US Navy's PRIDE electronic warfare suite (which also includes the ALR-45 and ALR-50 warning receivers), it was based on the ALQ-100. An updated version known as the ALQ-126B is now available as a direct replacement for the basic -126, but its installation will probably be limited to older USN fighter and attack

aircraft. It will be teamed with the Northrop ALQ-162 CW jammer, Itek ALR-45 and APR-43 RWRs, and the Tracor ALE-39 countermeasures dispenser, creating an EW suite suitable for all USN aircraft not due to receive the new and highly sophisticated ALQ-165. The latter is due for installation on the F-14D, but it is possible that the F-14A might use the -126B and -162 combination.

Testing of all these electronic systems is carried out on board carriers and at shore sites by means of the USM-247 Versatile Avionics Shop Test (VAST) system. Based around a UNIVAC 1240 computer, this automatic test equipment incorporates a tape-control unit, data transfer unit, plus the electronics needed to generate electronic stimuli under the control of the computer, and to check for correct responses from the equipment under test. VAST entered USN service in 1971. Operating for up to 20 hours per day, the USN's systems have long exceeded 1,000,000 hours of operational service. Being automatic, they reduce the number of highly trained technicians needed to handle avionics repair tasks, while the high repair turnaround times resulting from automatic test techniques reduce the amount of spares which must be stocked. Avionics units spend more time in the air, and less time on the shelf.

Chapter 3
F-14 in action

Having built and flight tested Tomcat, Grumman now faced the task of getting the aircraft built in large numbers and delivered to the US Navy. As aircraft moved down the line, and the programme gathered speed, all was well on the technical front, but behind the scenes a crisis was developing which would not only threaten the future of the programme, but of Grumman itself.

The initial contract signed back in 1969 covered 12 prototypes, but included options for 429 production fighters at an agreed price. This sort of fixed-price contract was in vogue at the time, and was another innovation of the McNamara era. In practice, the concept was a disaster. All the major aircraft programmes managed under this philosophy were to hit problems. The Lockheed C-5 Galaxy required an expensive wing rebuild half way through its service life, most of the USAF's F-111s were to be built before the design was fully mature, and the Tomcat deal almost drove Grumman out of the aircraft business.

Under the deal signed with the DoD, fixed prices were established for the aircraft over a seven year period. These annual options under which the DoD could purchase aircraft at agreed prices assumed an annual inflation rate of 3 per cent, a figure which was not open to adjustment until near the end of this time period. In practice, galloping inflation was to hit the economy of the US and most of the Western world. As the cost of labour and materials continued to rise, fixed prices became increasingly unrealistic. At the same time, cutbacks in other Grumman military and space programmes increased the overhead costs which the F-14 was required to carry.

In March 1971, Grumman came to the not unreasonable conclusion that the existing contract was unworkable, and asked the USN to re-negotiate the deal. This request was turned down by the Navy and DoD. A fixed price had been agreed, and a fixed price was going to be paid. A year later, company chairman E Clinton Towl told the Senate Tactical Air Power Subcommittee that if the USN continued to insist on the fixed prices beyond the fifth production batch, the company could no longer afford to continue with the F-14 programme, and would be forced to 'close its doors'. The company clocked up a deficit of $18 million in 1971, and no less than $70 million in 1972, so action was urgently needed.

The DoD finally agreed to re-negotiate, and a compromise was reached in March 1973 under which Grumman would observe the fixed price for the first 134 production aircraft, accepting that for the next two years the price paid for the aircraft would fall 20 per cent short of the actual costs which the company would incur, and that the company would as a result make a $220 million loss. The Navy agreed to re-

OVERLEAF
Early production Tomcats on the Calverton flight line. These early aircraft were the subject of a controversial fixed-price contract, and led to Grumman making a heavy loss in the initial stages of the Tomcat programme (Grumman)

negotiate the price of follow-on Tomcats, and to provide Grumman with a $200 million loan to tide the company over until the re-negotiated prices took effect.

This agreement was bound to stir up controversy. Grumman was even accused of investing the USN loan money in short-term US Government securities in order to make a profit of $2.8 million—a charge which overlooked the fact that Grumman could not instantly spend the funding as it was received, but could only spend it as required to settle bills. Such short-term investment of temporarily surplus cash was normal business practice, the company pointed out, and the interest received was well below that being charged by the Navy to Grumman.

In August 1974 Congress decided to terminate the loan, plunging Grumman into trouble once again. By this time the company had another customer—Iran had just placed an order for 80 Tomcats. Iran proved more understanding than the US Congress, with

OPPOSITE TOP
As one airframe is 'tortured' in the fatigue test rig, another takes shape in the foreground. The load carrying wing box and its pivots may be clearly seen on the latter aircraft (Grumman)

OPPOSITE BOTTOM
At Calverton, the various sub-assemblies are united with the fuselage to create a recognizable Tomcat. The early-pattern 'beaver tail' shows that this is an early production example. Note the dense electrical cabling in the spine (Grumman)

BELOW
Tomcat fuselages take shape on the Bethpage production line (Grumman)

ABOVE
Not the most dignified way of boarding a carrier for the first time, but probably the safest—the No 11 aircraft is hoisted prior to being lifted aboard the carrier Independence *on 22 March 1972*

RIGHT
Ground crew manoeuvre the No 11 aircraft on the deserted flight deck of Independence, *positioning it on the No 4 catapult. Such handling tests form an important part of early carrier compatibility trials*

Bank Melli stepping in to provide a $75 million loan. With this backing, Grumman was able to approach US banks, and a consortium of nine finally agreed to lend the remaining $125 million. With the future of the F-14 and Grumman now assured, the company was able to turn in profits of $17 million and $20 million in 1973 and 1974, and in 1975 Tomcat finally began to make money for the company.

By this time the aircraft was in service. The readiness unit and the first two squadrons were formed at Naval Air Station (NAS) Mirimar in California. Fleet Readiness Squadron VF-124 received its first F-14 in June 1972. The first two operational Tomcat units were VF-1 'Wolfpack' and VF-2 'Bounty Hunters' which commissioned at NAS Miramar on 14 October 1972. Almost two years later they deployed aboard the USS *Enterprise*. The only modification required to aircraft carriers was the installation of new jet blast deflectors, which were added during routine overhauls.

Tomcat was in service just in time to see the closing stages of the Vietnam war, flying top cover for the helicopter fleet used to evacuate US personnel from Saigon within hours of the final collapse of South Vietnam. With final victory assured, the North Vietnamese Air Force made no attempt to tangle with the new fighter, although one Tomcat did receive minor damage from anti-aircraft fire.

While Miramar trained squadrons on the West coast, a second training establishment was set up at NAS Oceana in Virginia. Creating these establishments was not just a matter of sending men and machines to a suitable base. Specialized ground facilities had to be provided, including simulators which would permit classroom training for aircrew and technicians. NAS Miramar and NAS Oceana each have two operational flight trainers, one weapon system trainer, two cockpit procedures trainers, and two part-task trainers.

The Grumman operational flight trainer includes all the flight instruments of the F-14 including the VDIG (Vertical Display Indicator Group) and datalink system, plus an aircraft motion system able to provide the trainee with the sensations of flight. It is used for familiarization training, and for intensive training in operational procedures, navigation, and communications.

Developed by Singer-Link, the weapon systems trainer duplicates the tactical environment within which the F-14 flies and fights. Missions may be simulated, including catapult launch from the carrier deck, en-route navigation, the detection of SAM threats, the use of the Tomcat's ECM equipment and weaponry, and the return to the carrier and subsequent recovery. Even the cockpit noises associated with the activation of aircraft systems or weapons are reproduced.

The Gould-developed cockpit procedural trainer provides realistic pilot training in cockpit familiarization, plus normal, emergency, and ground pro-

ABOVE RIGHT
As Tanzanian troops invaded Uganda in 1977 to depose dictator Idi Amin, both superpowers were watching. This Soviet Il-38 May maritime patrol aircraft was intercepted by Tomcats of VF-2 from the carrier Enterprise. *The US carrier was on patrol in the Indian Ocean; the Il-38 had probably flown from an airbase in South Yemen (US Navy)*

OPPOSITE
A VF-1 'Wolfpack' aircraft is directed to the catapult aboard Enterprise
(Grumman)

TOMCAT

*By keeping their wings in the oversweep position, two
aircraft of VF-142 'Ghost Riders' occupy a minimum of
deck space on* America *as a third runs-up its TF30
turbofans for take-off*
(Grumman)

OVERLEAF
*Tomcat of VF-2 'Bounty Hunters' at Naval Air Station
Miramar, California*
(Grumman)

96

ABOVE
Flight deck personnel are trained to react quickly to any incident or emergency. As the firefighters stand by, a tug pulls an aircraft with a burst starboard tyre to safety. This slick recovery operation is the end product of long hours of training
(US Navy via Robert F Dorr)

OPPOSITE
Carrier trials aboard Forrestal. *The aircraft is on the catapult, the jet deflector is raised, the afterburner nozzles are fully open, but the position of the flight deck crew indicate that launch is not imminent*
(Grumman)

cedures for the F-14. It also allows technicians to be trained in maintenance procedures such as engine trim checks and adjustment. By interconnecting the operational flight trainer with the part task trainer the pilot's AWG-9 system controls and displays may be activated.

Modifying and updating these trainers is a continuing task. Around 1980 the USN spent over $20 million on upgrades, while recent modifications have added new computers and equipment to match recent avionics changes to the aircraft such as the expanded memory AWG-9 computer. More drastic rebuilds will be needed to match this equipment to the new F-14D standard.

First east coast squadron to become operational on Tomcat were VF-14 'Tophatters'. In June 1975 the Atlantic Fleet received its first F-14s when this unit and VF-32 'Swordsmen' put to sea aboard the *Kennedy*. During a Mediterranean cruise, the unit scored a 100 per cent kill rate during missile-firing exercises. This unit was the first to have all its aircraft equipped with the Northrop-developed TV sensor.

Third carrier to receive Tomcats was *America*, which started a deployment with VF-142 'Ghostriders' and VF-143 'The World Famous Pukin' Dogs' embarked in April 1976. *Constellation* was next, acting as base for VF-24 'Fighting Renegades' and VF-211 'Fighting Checkmates' from September 1977 onwards. *Kitty Hawk* deployed a month later with VF-114 and VF-213, *Nimitz* in December with VF-41 'Black Aces' and VF-84 'Jolly Rogers'.

The F-14A was now a powerful component of USN fighter strength. The next five carriers to re-equip were:

CV-64	Constella-tion	April 1977	VF-142	VF-143
CV-63	Kitty Hawk	October 1977	VF-114	VF-213
CVN-68	Nimitz	December 1977	VF-41	VF-84
CVN-69	Eisenhower	January 1979	VF-142	VF-143
CV-61	Ranger	September 1980	VF-1	VF-2

'Big John' at speed: the mobile air power embarked on the
John F Kennedy *is beyond the pocket of most nations*
(Grumman)

As conversions continued, Tomcat squadrons found themselves being assigned to the older carriers. For these vessels, deployment of Tomcat was not so simple. CV-60 *Saratoga* was more than 15 years old when faced with the prospect of operating the new fighter. The first US carrier to undergo a Service Life Extension Program, *Saratoga* was surrendered to the Naval Shipyard at Philadelphia on 8 October 1980 to begin a $549.1 million rebuild. Changes to the vessel included a 42 ft (12.8 m) catapult extension, beefing up the deck-edge elevators to handle 110,000 lb (50,000 kg) loads instead of 84,000 lb (38,000 kg), and the addition of new storerooms in the fantail area, and the provision of a new elevator to handle the Phoenix missile.

The performance of the new fighter was a major improvement on that of the F-4 Phantom it replaced. Simple parameters such as top speed and combat ceiling were still in the Phantom class, but in range, manoeuvrability and firepower, Tomcat was in a class by itself.

Early in the flight-test programme it became obvious that the result was going to be an impressive aircraft. Compared with the best existing USN fighters the Tomcat offered a 21 per cent increase in rate of acceleration and sustained G-force, 20 per cent increase in rate of climb, 27 per cent increase in manoeuvring climb capability, and a 40 per cent improvement in turn radius.

When the aircraft is ready to set out on a mission, the starboard engine is started first. Once external air and power are disconnected, the port engine is then started using air bled from the starboard engine. The computer carries out a pre-flight checkout routine which tests 25 aircraft subsystems, including the variable-geometry inlet systems, air-data computer, stability-augmentation system, and navaids. Faults can be isolated to LRU level.

On board a carrier, Tomcat taxies with the wings swept. Moving the wings to the forward position increases the span by around 31 ft (9.5 m) so the wings are kept swept to ease manoeuvring on the flight deck. Only as the aircraft approaches the catapult do the crew bring the wings to the forward position.

OPPOSITE
The Tomcats at the aft end of Kennedy's *flight deck demonstrate how the wing oversweep position eases congestion. The rectangular box just below the port side of the flight deck is a launcher for the Sea Sparrow point-defence missile system*
(Grumman)

BELOW
Final checks before the catapult is fired during Tomcat compatibility tests aboard Forrestal *in November 1973*
(US Navy via Robert F Dorr)

ABOVE
Steam leaks from the catapult track as a VF-101 'Grim Reapers' aircraft moves forward to position itself for launch. The wings are still swept back (Grumman)

OPPOSITE TOP
Wreathed in catapult steam, a Tomcat of VF-33 'Tarsiers' waits on the deck of America while a ground crewman clambers up the fuselage side to hastily confer with the pilot (Grumman)

OPPOSITE BOTTOM
As the US evacuated personnel from Saigon in April 1975, the newly deployed Tomcats of VF-2 on Enterprise were available to fly top cover for the airlift. This Tomcat is climbing away without reheat, indicating a practice touchdown (US Navy via Robert F Dorr)

Turning radius is small, thanks to the ample degree of nose steering available, and is 70 degrees in either direction.

Normal take-off procedure from a land runway is to position the aircraft in take-off configuration, with the wing fully forward and the flaps and slats at full deflection. The flaps are in three sections—two-section main flaps and a smaller inboard auxiliary flap. The latter is only completely clear of the glove when the wing is fully forward, so a system of interlocks prevents auxiliaries being lowered unless the wing is fully forward, or the wing being moved from the fully-forward position while the auxiliaries are down. Full down positions for the slats and flaps are 17 degrees and 35 degrees respectively.

The engines are run up to military power, engine instruments are checked, then the pilot goes to maximum afterburner and releases the brakes. At full thrust, the brakes cannot hold the aircraft—the tyres would simply skid. Acceleration is rapid. At around 100 knots, the pilot eases back the control column. This movement must not be taken to its limits—full back stick would cause the horizontal stabilizer to stall, increasing the take-off run by several hundred feet. As soon as the nose rises, Tomcat lifts off. Minimum take-off distance is around 1,200 ft (366 m).

For a carrier launch, the pilot must trim the aircraft to match its gross weight. The pilot steers the aircraft to the catapult, and the crew make the necessary connection. The F-4 Phantom was catapulted with its nose strut extended, so it had to be linked to the catapult using a cable, but the F-14 is launched in a 'kneeling' position, with the nose strut compressed. No cables are needed. Once the throttles have been advanced to take-off power, a detent on the throttle control locks them at this position. Known as the Catapult Detent, this prevents the throttles being jerked backwards under acceleration as the aircraft is catapulted. The pilot does not hold the control column for take-off, he merely restrains it with his hand. When ready to go, he signals to the Catapult Officer, then puts his head back into the headrest to await the firing of the catapult. As the catapult completes its stroke, the energy contained in the compressed nose strut pitches the aircraft into the correct flying attitude.

Once Tomcat is airborne, flaps and undercarriage must be retracted. If the aircraft is not put into a climb, this must be done right away. Undercarriage retraction takes around 10 seconds, and the aircraft's fast acceleration will soon bring it to 280 knots—the highest speed at which the gear may be extended.

Most aircraft only manage to look futuristic in the manufacturer's earliest artists impressions, but as this VF-102 'Diamondbacks' from America *shows, the F-14 still looks every inch a modern fighter more than a decade after entering front-line service*
(Grumman)

Maximum speed with flaps extended is 225 knots; the flaps are structurally cleared to 280 knots, but Grumman has left the earlier figure in the pilot's manual to encourage the crew to retract them as soon as possible. On most sorties, afterburner can then be cancelled, the aircraft cruising in dry thrust. Sea-level rate of climb is more than 35,000 ft per minute (10,660 m/min).

Handling

Tomcat is easy to fly. The F-4 Phantom could prove tricky to manoeuvre at low level, and many were lost in spins. The USN was determined to avoid such problems with its new fighter. Stalling speed is 103 knots, and test flights have shown that control may be maintained at speeds of down to 105 knots. With the wings fully forward, the F-14 is impossible to stall. With full wing sweep, the aircraft can be flown at angles of attack from +90 to −50 degrees. The latter figure does not represent a dive, but the result of rolling inverted then pushing the stick forward to put Tomcat into a climb.

Given a high throttle setting, Tomcat may be 'stood on its tail', holding a steady angle of around 77 degrees. At full sweep, Tomcat is spin-proof, says Grumman, while at a 22 degree sweep angle a spin may only be initiated by using the differential tail. This impressive performance is partly due to the lift generated by the lower surface, particularly the rear area between the engine bays.

Stability augmentation systems (SAS) are fitted to pitch, roll and yaw axes. Tomcat is very stable in pitch, and can be flown over the entire performance envelope with the pitch SAS turned off. The unit has only a modest effect on handling qualities. The roll SAS is of much greater significance, and limits the roll rate. Maximum deflection of the differentially-moving stabilizers is nominally seven degrees up and seven degrees down, but the roll SAS may limit this or even demand up to 5 degrees more deflection. The yaw SAS improves directional stability, and co-ordinates the roll of the aircraft. An engine failure at high speed will create a strong tendency to yaw in the direction of the failed engine, but the yaw SAS can deflect the rudders by up to 19 degrees to keep the aircraft flying straight ahead.

Early variable-geometry aircraft used manually-controlled wings. On the F-111, the original design was such that the wing-sweep control worked in the same sense as a throttle—for maximum speed the control was pushed forward, while the wings moved backward. Tomcat was the first VG aircraft to use an automatic system. As Mach number varies, the air-data computer automatically moves the wing to the position which will give the optimum lift/drag ratio, and thus optimum turning performance.

Normal sweep range is from 20 to 68 degrees. The 'oversweep' position of 75 degrees is used only on the ground or on a carrier, having been provided to

OPPOSITE TOP
When this clean VF-84 'Jolly Rogers' aircraft lights the afterburners, the thrust and drag curves will not meet until well beyond Mach 2
(Gruman)

OPPOSITE BOTTOM
In a computerized wargame played by the author during the research for this book, Tomcats launched in mid-Atlantic from Nimitz *(seen here in real life with a VF-84 low-speed escort) flew non-stop to the UK to boost Britain's shattered fighter defences, while others disposed of most of a Soviet task force's Yakovlev Yak-38* Forger *fighters in only two engagements. Soviet readers will be glad to learn that AS-6 armed Tu-16 and Tu-22M bombers had their own 'turkey shoot' in the days of game time which followed. The naval convoy which* Nimitz *was escorting made it to the UK, but suffered disastrous losses on the way*
(Gruman)

ABOVE
Lt Bullet Richardson (no relation to the author) tucks in close to the chase plane during a VF-211 'Flying Checkmates' sortie. The tip of an AIM-9 Sidewinder may be seen just ahead of the starboard wing glove

minimize the space required by a parked aircraft. Original F-14 plans assumed that the aircraft would be used for ground attack. Had this plan been pursued, a fixed 55 degree sweep angle would have been used for bomb, gun or unguided rocket attacks. At this angle, maximum structural rigidity would be obtained, and one variable (sweep angle) would be eliminated from weapon-delivery calculations. The wing sweep control selector still has a BOMB position, but this is never used.

Wing sweep is normally handled automatically, a significant advantage in combat, particularly in the subsonic Mach 0.6–0.9 speed range typical of dogfight engagements. This gives the aircraft a valuable performance edge over many other VG types. The pilot of the MiG-23 has no such refinements, and must manually select one of three positions—low speed (forward), intermediate, or high-speed (fully-swept).

A manual sweep-angle control is also fitted. This works the same way as the wing movement being demanded—control forward for wing forward, control back for maximum sweep—but a sensing system is provided to ensure that structural limits are

The glove vanes, seen here in the extended position, are normally deployed only at supersonic speed (Grumman)

not exceeded. Maximum wing angle is determined by the computer, based on flight conditions. Up to Mach 0.4 for example, the maximum permissable angle is only 22 degrees—only two degrees more than the 20 degree unswept position. In the event of the pilot attempting to select an excessively-low sweep angle while his aircraft is travelling at high speed, the flight-control system will limit the angle which may be set.

The only time that pilots are likely to override the automatic system is in formation flying, when the high sweep permits a tighter formation, and in order to lose speed before landing. (Set to maximum sweep, the wing has high induced drag which can be used to bleed off speed). Once the speed is right, flipping a throttle-mounted selector switch back to AUTO mode restores control to the automatic system, which brings the wings forward to the 20 degree position for landing.

The wing incorporates plain trailing-edge flaps, full-span leading-edge slats, lift dumpers, and

Fresh from the Calverton paint shop—the canopy is still masked—the prototype F-14 (buno 157980) makes its debut. Its career was cut short when it crashed approaching Calverton Field during its second flight on 30 December 1970. Chief test pilot Robert Smythe and project pilot William 'Bob' Millar ejected successfully—but only just (Grumman)

LEFT ABOVE
Before the second prototype was allowed to fly on 24 May 1971, its titanium hydraulic lines were replaced with steel pipes, and the revised system was put through a series of rigorous ground tests. The No 2 Tomcat investigated low-speed, high-lift portions of the flight envelope, and is seen here with its gear down, wings fully forward (with full-span flaps and slats extended), and airbrake raised. The original 'beaver tail' is also evident
(Grumman)

LEFT BELOW
Every F-14 ever built has been fitted with Martin-Baker GRU-7A ejection seats. The F-14D will be equipped with the NACES (navy aircrew common ejection seat) which will also be manufactured by Martin-Baker and installed in A-6, T-45, and F-18 aircraft. During clearance trials before the prototype made its first flight, a rear-seat ejection is scrutinzed by high-speed ciné cameras
(Grumman)

ABOVE
An AIM-7 Sparrow 'snaps-down' after launch from a Tomcat of VF-84, the 'Jolly Rogers'. This semi-active radar missile is used at intermediate ranges, with the smaller AIM-9 Sidewinder taking over at short range. Hughes' AIM-120A AMRAAM is scheduled to supersede the Sparrow in the 1990s
(Grumman)

LEFT ABOVE
The F-14B prototype was to have been the first example of the definitive Tomcat. Its Pratt & Whitney F401 turbofans were based on the F100 used by the USAF's F-15 Eagle, and later by the F-16 Fighting Falcon. This Tomcat has had a short flying career—Congress decided to terminate development of the F401 engine—and the airplane was placed in storage. It was dusted-off to be used as a testbed for the F101DFE, becoming the 'Super Tomcat' until it was converted into the F-14D prototype and fitted with General Electric F110 turbofans
(Grumman)

F-14A Tomcats of VF-33 'Tarsiers' parked on the deck of USS America (CV-66) in July 1984
(Jean-Pierre Montbazet)

LEFT
In designing the Tomcat, Mike Pelehach and his team took care to locate the engines in nacelles well clear of the fuselage. The stall-prone TF30 turbofans (seen here in partial afterburner) thus received a near-optimum airflow undisturbed by boundary layer turbulence. This aircraft is armed with six AIM-54 Phoenix AAMs
(Grumman)

This close-up of a Tomcat 'six-pack' shows the wing oversweep used to maximize deck parking space
(Jean-Pierre Montbazet)

RIGHT ABOVE
With its crew strapped in and ready to go, F-14A Tomcat
of VF-74 'Be-Devilers' waits to taxi along the deck prior
to being launched from USS Saratoga (CV-60) in August
1984. The Tomcat in the foreground, side number 211,
belongs to VF-103 'Sluggers' and wears an experimental
gray scheme
(Jean-Pierre Montbazet)

RIGHT BELOW
F-14A Tomcat of VF-84 'Jolly Rogers' set up for a
catapult shot from the USS Nimitz (CVN-68) in January
1983. VF-84 have resisted the change to low visibility
squadron markings and retain their colourful 'skull and
crossbones' motif on the fins
(Jean-Pierre Montbazet)

The deck crews take cover and prepare to withstand the
violence of a catapult launch. This F-14A of VF-103
'Sluggers' is cleared for take-off from the Saratoga in
August 1984
(Jean-Pierre Montbazet)

F-14A, side number 201, of VF-103 'Sluggers', blasts off
assisted by one of Sara's bow cats
(Jean-Pierre Montbazet)

ABOVE
Two F-14s share the port side deck-edge lift as others fly overhead. The art of parking aircraft with their tails over the deck and elevator edge is a delicate one. Sudden severe rolls have sent more than one USN aircraft tumbling overboard!
(Grumman)

BELOW
Carriers are the ideal operating base for aircraft supporting limited operations, as the recent US involvement in Lebanon showed. With Beirut airport often under fire, the Lebanese Air Force effectively grounded, and the US Marines a target for snipers and suicide attacks, the carriers provided a safe haven for the Tomcats and A-7s which supported the beleaguered ground force
(Grumman)

spoilers. Primary method of roll control is by differential deflection of the horizontal tail surfaces, supplemented by the wing-mounted spoilers. The tail surfaces always contributes to roll control, but have little effect at low speeds where the spoilers are much more effective. The latter are used at wing angles of less than 57 degrees.

For air combat manoeuvring, the flaps and slats may be deployed in an intermediate position designed to give maximum turn rate. The slats are set to around 7 degrees, the flaps to 10 degrees. The wing must be positioned between 20 and 50 degrees, and the inboard auxiliary flaps are not involved. As with wing sweep, deployment of the flaps and slats to the manoeuvring position is done automatically by the flight control system. As the aircraft angle of attack exceeds a defined limit, and is within a pre-defined Q (dynamic pressure) limit, the surfaces are deployed, retracting again once the AOA falls back below the limit. Manual control is also available using a thumbwheel on the control column, but this will not allow the surfaces to be extended if this would result

in damage. Like wing sweep, this slat and flap deployment would normally be trusted to the automatic system. In combat a pilot is unlikely to have the time to worry about wing and slat/flap positions. Even if he did, he lacks the detailed data needed in order to make best use of them.

If the pilot is tracking a target in air combat, he would hardly welcome having his aim thrown off by the effects of flap and slat deployment, so the aircraft's Integrated Trim System offsets the pitching moments which result from the slats and flaps being moved by adjusting the angle of the horizontal stabilizer.

The glove-mounted vanes are deployed between

ABOVE
Close-up of the tailhook
(Jean-Pierre Montbazet)

BELOW
The moment of touchdown on America *for a Tomcat of VF-102 'Diamondbacks'. The tailhook has picked up the wire, but the latter is not yet taut. The jetpipe nozzles are closed, indicating dry thrust, and the tail-mounted airbrake is deployed*
(Grumman)

A moment of excitement aboard Kitty Hawk *as a Tomcat of VF-51 'Screaming Eagles' blows a tyre on touchdown. Note the extended slats and flaps on the wing (US Navy via Robert F Dorr)*

Afterburners at full power, a Tomcat of VF-32 'Swordsman' prepares for a night catapult shot (Grumman)

Mach 1 and Mach 1.4. Above Mach 1.4 they will gradually retract from the fully-deployed 15 degree position, reaching the full-in state at Mach 1.5. By offsetting the movement of the centre of pressure as the aircraft goes supersonic, they offset the increase in stability which would otherwise be experienced at such speeds, maintaining Tomcat's turning performance. They also deploy at intermediate sweep angles of between 35 and 50 degrees when the manoeuvring flap setting is selected in an attempt to give extra lift, but their effect in this secondary role is minimal. They will also deploy if the fixed 55 degree sweep planned for air-to-ground use is selected.

When in cruising flight, pilots prefer to fly at low altitude, where Tomcat's handling qualities are at their best. With the wing swept back, the ride is pretty smooth, even at high speeds. Max cruising speed is 550 knots. Ultimate limits of the performance envelope include a top speed well above Mach 2. Maximum design speed is Mach 2.4, a figure to which Tomcat has been cleared in flight test, but the USN sets a lower limit of around Mach 2.25 for service aircrew. Service ceiling is 50,000 ft (15,240 m). In air combat, agility and acceleration are more important than theoretical limits which only a test pilot is likely to meet. Tomcat is agile in a dogfight—the aircraft can execute a 180 degree 6.5 G turn of 1,800 ft (550 m) radius in only 10 seconds without loss of speed. Tomcat can hold 6.5 G at Mach 2.2, or accelerate from loiter to Mach 1.8 in 75 seconds. From take-off to Mach 0.9 at low level, thrust will increase by around 30 per cent due to the ram effect. At Mach 0.9 and 10,000–15,000 ft (3000–4500 m) thrust to weight ratio is typically around unity with 50 per cent fuel remaining.

The USN wanted the F-14 to have a radius of action some 80 per cent greater than that of the F-4J, allowing a flight to a target area some 400 nm (740 km) away, followed by 2 minutes of combat at full afterburner at 10,000 ft (3000 m). Tests showed that the F-14A required only 14,250 lb of internal fuel in order to meet the USN requirement for a 500 nm combat radius on an air-superiority mission with four AIM-7 Sparrows and the internal gun. This figure was 2,250 lb (1020 kg) less than the 16,500 lb (7500 kg) which the airframe could carry, but Grumman opted to install the latter load, reasoning that this would ease the task of converting F-14As to the -14B configuration.

Loaded with four Phoenix, two Sparrows, two Sidewinders and two external tanks, the Tomcat can loiter on combat air patrol for 90 minutes at 150 nm (278 km) from the carrier, or for an hour at a range of 253 nm (470 km). On a deck-launched intercept mission with the same warload, tactical radius is 171 nm (317 km) with a Mach 1.3 flyout, or 134 nm (248 km) at Mach 1.5.

The canopy gives excellent visibility, both to the front, sides and rear, inducing negligible distortion. On some prototype aircraft, Grumman projected

*This view of the flight line at Naval Air Station Oceana
gives a good view of the air spillage doors on the upper
surface of the intakes. Originally controlled by an actuator,
they are now fixed open by a mechanical link. The aircraft
are from VF-14 'Tophatters'
(Grumman)*

The 72-degree oversweep position eases the problems of manoeuvring Tomcat on a crowded flight deck (via Lindsay Peacock)

HUD symbology directly onto the canopy rather than onto a combiner glass. The retractable refuelling probe is located on the starboard side of the fuselage, just ahead of the cockpit. This location gives good visibility when connecting to and disconnecting from the tanker's trailing drogue, but a US journalist from *Aviation Week* magazine who flew a back-seat sortie in the 11th prototype back in early 1973 noted that 'A great deal of noise is heard when the probe is extended into the airstream.'

On the approach, the aircraft will fly with the wings fully forward. Once the undercarriage is down and locked, the flaps are lowered. The interlock on the flaps prevents the auxiliary flaps from lowering unless the wing is fully forward. Should the wings not be fully forward when flaps are demanded, the fact that the auxiliaries have not lowered will be signalled to the pilot by a warning light. The tailhook would be lowered for a carrier landing, or kept up if coming into an airfield.

Several F-111 have been lost when the crew omitted to bring the wings forward for landing, circumstances which resulted in the aircraft stalling on final approach. On the F-14, the automatic sweep control should keep the pilot safe, while the interlock between flaps and sweep angle provide another safety measure—the aircraft cannot be configured for landing unless the wings are fully forward. With the

wing set to 55 degrees or greater, the flap handle cannot be moved unless the wings have been moved forward. Once the wing is forward of the 50 degree position, the handle will move and the main flaps will lower, but the crew will be warned that the auxiliaries are still raised.

Approaches are flown with the speed brakes out. This allows the engine to operate at a higher RPM than if the aircraft were clean, ensuring a fast engine response should the pilot suddenly select military thrust or even afterburner in the event of a wave-off by the carrier, or some sudden emergency.

In order to satisfy carrier-landing requirements, Grumman devised a direct-lift control system which uses the wing spoilers. On the approach, Tomcat would have maintained a constant 10.8 degree angle of attack, with the spoilers free to move by up to five

OVERLEAF
Carrier hangars are rarely as uncrowded as this, but Tomcat's carrier-suitability trials aboard Forrestal *in December 1973 were a special occasion for the US Navy and the aircraft was given VIP treatment (US Navy via Robert F Dorr)*

*The world's finest naval fighter meets what many would
regard as the world's finest maritime patrol aircraft—the
British Aerospace Nimrod
(Grumman)*

*Grumman E-2C Hawkeyes and A-6 Intruders may not be
the ideal flying companions for any VF-213 'Black Lions'
pilot wishing to display The Right Stuff of which fighter
pilots are proud, but this unusual formation demonstrates
the leading position which Grumman holds in the field of
carrier-borne aviation. The company provides the US
Navy with its long range eyes, teeth, and heavy punch
(Grumman)*

degrees. Approach speed depends on the gross weight of the aircraft. With around 4,000 lb (1800 kg) of fuel remaining, speed would typically be around 120 knots. Carrier landings are carried out at a constant angle of attack, and thus a constant rate of sink, and this technique is also used for landing on runways. Grumman's Calverton flight test facility is equipped with a carrier-type mirror sight which the pilots use on the approach. Minimum landing distance on a runway is 1,600 ft (488 m).

Loss of an engine in flight is no big problem. Even with a single TF30, Tomcat has enough thrust to make a normal approach. In the event of a double-engine failure, the crew must restart at least one. Tomcat cannot make a deadstick landing, since hydraulic pressure will be lost once the engines spool down and stop. The F-14A does not have an emergency ram-air turbine. This fits in with current US Navy operating procedures. Aircrew did train in deadstick landing techniques, but the service eventually realized that damage to an aircraft caused by such a tricky manoeuvre completely outweighed the value of the aircraft saved by deadstick landings. Current doctrine calls for crews who suffer total engine failure to eject rather than attempt a landing.

One problem which was to plague the F-14A was the reliability of its TF30 engine. In a way, Tomcat's magnificent handling qualities made life difficult for the propulsion system—the sort of high angles of

attack, yawing moments and low airspeeds which the aircraft can cope with are hardly conducive to smooth engine operation.

Initially the Tomcat's widely-spaced nacelles seemed to have cured the problems which affected the TF30 turbofan when used in the F-111. More than 100 aircraft had been delivered and 30,000 flying hours logged when the first engine incident occurred in April 1974. On several occasions, fan blades broke free. The original requirement had not specified that the engine casing should retain a loose blade, so the end result was damage to the surrounding structure and systems.

After losing two aircraft from *Enterprise* to engine problems, the US Navy decided in early 1975 to remove the engines after every 100 flying hours, open the compressor casings and inspect the fan sections, bleed ducts and fuel lines. After these checks, the engines were re-assembled, run in a test cell, then refitted to the aircraft. More than 50 engines were to pass through this teardown procedure in a two-month period while the carrier remained on station in the Indian Ocean.

By the summer of 1975 five such incidents had occurred. Four resulted in onboard fires, two in the loss of the aircraft. Action was clearly needed. P&W reported that the problem lay in blades supplied by a vendor, so the Navy ordered that the fan blades of all 145 aircraft delivered to date be inspected.

ABOVE
F-14A buno 159433 with intake guards in place
(Robert F Dorr)

ABOVE
In the mid-1970s, Tomcat was the star attraction at many air shows. This aircraft from VF-124 'Gunfighters' visited the 1976 Iruma Air Show in Japan
(Robert F Dorr)

LEFT
Formation flying for air-to-air photography can be dangerous, so the back seater of this VF-1 'Wolfpack' aircraft has turned to keep an eye on the photographic aircraft
(Grumman)

By January 1977 P&W was delivering the improved TF30-P-414. Rated at 20,900 lb (9480 kg) this incorporated modifications intended to prevent blade cracking and to contain any blade failures. New compressor blades were made from a revised titanium alloy and with increased leading-edge radius, while the fan case was strengthened. Engineering Change Proposals 835, 853 and 854 tackled the problems of engine related fires. These included adding a fire-extinguishing system and ablative coatings in the nacelle area, and were introduced by July 1977.

Despite these changes, engine problems continued. US Navy officials blamed the TF30 powerplants for contributing significantly to aircraft losses. The fixes were directed at the blade-containment problem, but did little to help with the TF30's other major weakness—a tendency to stall.

'Compressor stall may occur at any altitude/airspeed combination,' the F-14A pilot's manual warns, but experience has shown that the engine is most troublesome at high altitudes, low speeds, and when lighting or cancelling afterburner. 'Subsonic compressor stalls are characterized by a thump or bang, an RPM decrease, and an increase in TIT (Turbine Inlet Temperature). At low speed or high AOA, rapid yaw rate or nose slice may be the first indication. Some stalls are quiet (usually stalls that occur at low power or high altitude) and cannot be heard by the aircrew.' Pilots were cautioned to check for indications of a stall immediately after missile firing. 'Supersonic compressor stalls are characterized by a bang, slight increase in TIT, and slow RPM decay. If the stall hangs (which they will normally do) the inlet will buzz.'

In some cases the engine recovers immediately, returning to normal operation. Stalls which 'hang' require the pilot to take action. The suggested recovery tactic was first to reduce any G loading on the aircraft in order to reduce the risk of departure into a spin, and to provide a near-normal airflow into the engine inlet. Retarding the throttles to IDLE minimized the assymetric thrust, a move which might take priority if the aircraft were to be yawing

violently. Since the combustor flame does not extinguish during a stall, the engine—deprived of its normal airflow—could overheat and be damaged. To prevent this, the engine throttle has to be moved to OFF, extinguishing the combustor flame and thereby reducing turbine blade temperature.

At supersonic speeds, the procedure is slightly different. The throttles are retarded as before, but the pilot must take greater care to avoid spin departure. Inlet buzz (the result of oscillations of the inlet duct's shock-wave system) occurs at a rate of around 6 Hz (six cycles per second) and can give the aircrew a rough and bumpy ride until ended by loss of speed at around Mach 1.2. It is not necessary to move the throttles to OFF; at supersonic speeds the airflow through the engine is sufficient to cool the turbine.

With the stall cleared, a windmill restart may be carried out if sufficient speed, altitude and hydraulic pressure are available. The alternative is to carry out a spool-down airstart as soon as the TIT temperature is within acceptable limits.

In 1976 and 1978, the average rate of compressor stalls was two per 1,000 flight hours. This fell to

LEFT
Tomcats on patrol—aircraft of VF-1 'Wolfpack' (left), VF-2 'Bounty Hunters' (centre) and VF-51 'Screaming Eagles' (right). All three are unarmed, but the empty Phoenix missile launchers under the belly (seen below the aft cockpit) create a distinctive outline (Grumman)

BELOW
This novel paint scheme was devised by artist Keith Ferris as a method of breaking up the visual outline of aircraft. This Tomcat (seen here at Naval Air Station Miramar in April 1977) is buno 158979 of VF-1 'Wolfpack' (R Besecker Collection via Robert F Dorr)

ABOVE
*Although the 'Bounty Hunters' of VF-2 were happy to try
the Ferris paint scheme, it was never adopted for service
(Duane A Kasulka via Robert F Dorr)*

BELOW
Plan view of two Tomcats in the Ferris camouflage scheme

A crowded hangar deck aboard Enterprise. *The aircraft in the foreground is from VF-2 'Bounty Hunters'*
(Grumman)

OPPOSITE TOP
Most training missions are uneventful—this F-14A is not even armed—but several sorties have resulted in aircraft being fired upon
(Grumann)

OPPOSITE BELOW
Grey seas and slippery wet flight deck—Tomcat defends the fleet in any weather. Aircraft is from VF-103 'Sluggers', looking good for the second wire on Saratoga
(Jean-Pierre Montbazet)

around 1.5 in 1979 and around 1 in 1980, but the problem still led to the loss of aircraft. The problem was probably exacerbated by a Navy decision to alter the F-14 training syllabus by insisting that full afterburner be used for all F-14 take-offs. If fuel puddled in the augmentor, delaying ignition, the mild explosion produced when the fuel ignited could travel forward through the fan face, reaching the face of the compressor and causing a stall. The variable nozzle was programmed not to open until ignition had been achieved, but P&W engineers investigated opening the nozzle slightly just before ignition, and looked at other methods of making the TF30 more tolerant of airflow distortions or hot-gas re-ingestion.

A TF30-P-414 improvement programme launched in Fiscal Year 1982 resulted in the current 414A. Repair, rework and redesign efforts carried out under a $50 million development contract are intended to reduce the incidence of engine stalls, and to increase low-cycle fatigue life, raising the intervals of time between hot section inspections and overhauls.

First -414A engines were delivered to the USN in 1983 for installation in the F-14 in 1984. As deliveries to Calverton began, TF30 programme manager

Donald Jorden claimed that the new engine was intended to eliminate restrictions on how the pilot uses engine power, allowing USN aircrew to fly the Tomcat through extreme angles of attack and manoeuvre without having to worry about engine stalls. The amount of visible exhaust smoke was also reduced. The company is convinced that the TF30 problems are at last cured, and offered the USN a warranty of 10 years or 3,000 hours on the first 95 new-built -414As delivered and the first 122 TF-30-414s retrofitted to the new -414A standard.

The saga of the TF30 has attracted many critics. In the summer of 1984, Navy Secretary John F Lehman described the F-14 installation as the 'worst mismatch in years', claiming that it was responsible for 28 per cent of the Tomcat crashes which had occurred by that time. Older F-14s are likely to run out of airframe life before an alternative engine is available, but a significant portion of the fleet is likely to be re-

ABOVE
Condensing water vapour reveals the position of the shock waves from a Tomcat flying at supersonic speed at low-level
(Grumman)

OPPOSITE
Tomcat may not have the thrust-to-weight ratio of the USAF's F-15 Eagle, but this 'Sundowner' shows what can be done even with TF30 power
(Grumman)

engined with the General Electric F110-400 power-plant developed for the follow-on F-14D.

On 14 September 1976, one of *Kennedy's* Tomcats hit the sea—and the newspaper headlines—when it rolled off the deck. The aircraft had gone out of control while taxiing to the catapult and headed for the edge of the flight deck. The pilot and RIO ejected at the last moment, but their mount ended up on the seabed 1,845 ft (560 m) below. At the time of the incident, *Kennedy* was operating in international waters 75 miles (120 km) northwest of the Orkney Islands, and the incident was witnessed by nearby Soviet Navy ships.

The West had only just been presented with a MiG-25 *Foxbat* thanks to the defection to Japan of Viktor Belenko, but was now faced with the possibility that the Soviet Union might retaliate by recovering the Tomcat. The US Navy decided to mount its own recovery operation. Within seven days of the incident, the first salvage vessels were on their way. A ten-day sonar search by the ocean-going tug *Shakori* finally located the aircraft, but worsening weather drove the vessel back to port. When the operation was resumed, the Tomcat was relocated on 14 September, but not at its original location.

Watched by Soviet ships, the US Navy's nuclear-powered NR-1 research sub dived to inspect the aircraft a week later. The reason for the change in position was soon revealed—the F-14 was festooned in a British fishing net, having been dragged across the ocean bed after being accidentally 'caught' by a trawler. Using a mechanical arm, NR-1 hooked a cable onto the aircraft's undercarriage, and the British-owned vessel *Oil Harrier* attempted to winch the Tomcat to the surface. The line snapped, so a stronger replacement was fitted and another lift was attempted. With the aircraft a mere 80 ft (24 m) from the surface, the line broke free, and the Tomcat returned to the seabed. While waiting for a better-equipped recovery vessel to reach the scene, the NR-1 recovered a Phoenix missile which had broken free from the aircraft.

When the West German vessels *Taurus* and *Twyford* finally made a firm attachment to the

ABOVE
TARPS produces high-quality imagery. This view of Carl
Vinson *(CVN-70) was taken by the pod's KA-99 camera
(US Navy, VF-111 via Grumman)*

BELOW
*Using the TARPS pod (seen here on flight test), US Navy
F-14s flew reconnaissance missions deep into Lebanese
airspace, drawing ground fire on several occasions in
support of US forces in Beirut
(Grumman)*

aircraft, it was lifted to within only 500 ft (225 m) of the surface, then held at that depth while *Taurus* steamed slowly back to the Orkneys and to relatively shallow and sheltered water, with its prize hanging below. Three miles (5 km) offshore and in water only 137 ft (42 m) deep and well within the operating range of conventional 'hard hat' divers, a better lifting line was attached, and the aircraft was hauled to the surface on 11 November, almost two months after leaving *Kennedy*'s deck. Total cost of the operation was $2.4 million.

On 5 October 1981 Cdr Jay Yakeley, commanding officer of VF-114 became the first F-14 pilot to clock up 2,000 flight hours on type. Involved with the Tomcat since 1973, he passed the 2,000 hour mark while operating from the carrier *America* during an Indian Ocean deployment. During the same month, Lt Chris Berg and Cdr Bill Bertsch of VF-24 each managed to register their 1,000th F-14 flying hour during the same flight and in the same aircraft while on a sortie from *Constellation*. Also in mid-1981, Capt John Waples of VF-2 became the USN's leading 'tailhooker' on active status when he made his 1,504th and 1,505th arrested landing while flying an F-14A from the carrier *Ranger*.

In the autumn of 1982, the conversion of VF-33 'Diamondbacks' and VF-102 'Tarsiers' from the F-4 to the F-14 raised the number of USN Tomcat squadrons to 20—18 operational units plus the two Fleet Readiness Squadrons. By now, conversion was a smooth process, taking around 11 months. VF-33 ended its last F-4 deployment from *America* on 6 June 1981 when the carrier finished an Indian Ocean cruise. On 10 May, they returned to *America* as an F-14 unit.

Tomcat is the US Navy's primary fleet-defence fighter, and the service plans to deploy two squadrons aboard every large-deck carrier. The USN originally planned to buy 344 aircraft, but this figure has steadily risen, first to 390 in FY74, then to 403 in FY77, and 521 in FY78. Current planning assumes a final total of 899, including 306 of the improved F-14D model. Tomcat remains an expensive aircraft. The original flyaway cost was $7.3 million, but by 1977 this had risen to around $12 million. Inflation has continued to bite, and the flyaway price for FY85 is now $32.7 million.

The production rate built up steadily during the early 1970s, peaking at more than 70 per year in FY75, 78, and 79. This figure was inflated by the assembly of aircraft for Iran; peak USN production rate was 50 per year in FY74 and 75. Since then the rate has dropped steadily, levelling off in FY83 at the

current 24 per year. Having made the decision to develop the improved F-14D version of the aircraft, the US Navy originally planned to close the F-14A line in fiscal years 1986, 1987 and 1988, re-opening it in FY89 to begin delivery of F-14Ds. Money saved by suspending production would have been used to help fund F-14D development. Grumman and a New York Congressional delegation successfully lobbied to have this decision re-considered, and in the late July 1983 it was agreed that the line would remain open at a low rate until the F-14D is ready. Planned production rate will be cut to 18 per annum in FY86 and FY87; purchases beyond this date will be of the F-14D.

Modifications to the existing fleet take up a rising portion of the USN budget. Since the early 1980s, it has risen from $43.4 million in FY81 to $241.7 million in FY85, and a scheduled $158.8 million in FY86. Current projects include:

Structural Improvements	($25.6 million)
Undercarriage upgrading	($11.6 million)
Weapons Rail modifications	($1.3 million)
TF30 engine modifications	($125.7 million)
Phoenix/AWG-9 Computer Expanded Memory	($12.2 million)
Improvements to aircraft wiring	($1.5 million)
Television Camera Sight	($17.4 million)

Tomcat forms a vital part of the US Navy's 'defence in depth' plans. USN anti-air warfare planning assumes that air thrusts must pass through three defensive zones—the outer defence zone, area defence zone and point defence zone. Defence in the outer zone is entrusted to the Tomcat/Phoenix combination, working in conjunction with airborne early-warning and electronic warfare aircraft. The goal is to detect and intercept bombers before the latter can launch air-to-surface missiles. Threats managing to break through this outer defence will enter the area defence zone and be engaged by missiles carried by anti-air warfare ships, most modern of which are the CG-47 *Ticonderoga*-class cruisers and the planned DDG-51 missile destroyers. 'Leakers' managing to survive Standard missile attack will be tackled by point-defence systems mounted on individual ships in the task force—systems such as Standard missiles, Phalanx 20 mm guns, and soft-kill systems such as jammers and decoys.

One role for which the F-14 was never designed was that of movie star, but the skull and crossbones emblazoned Tomcats of VF-84 'Jolly Rogers' and the

The introduction of the F-14 TARPS meant goodbye to the RF-8G Crusader and RA-5C Vigilante. The RF-8G pictured above, side number 604, buno 146845, served with VFP-306; RA-5C, side number 602, buno 156640, was assigned to RVAH-12 on the Saratoga (Robert F Dorr)

OVERLEAF
The TARPS infrared sensor captured these fascinating images of its Tomcat escort. The hot aft sections show white, as does the leakage of heat from around the seals at the aft edge of the wing glove. In the original print a considerable amount of detail may be seen in the aircraft's aft structure, with the thermal energy creating a X-ray-like image (Grumman)

carrier *Nimitz* starred in the 1980 motion picture *The Final Countdown*. More memorable for its spectacular flying sequences than for its somewhat unbelievable science-fiction plot, this shows *Nimitz* ('commanded' for the purposes of the film by actor Kirk Douglas) entering a 'time warp', only to find itself positioned off Pearl Harbor in December 1941 and excellently placed to engage the Japanese air strike. Fitted with wide-screen ciné cameras, several Tomcats were used to film air-to-air combat sequences, while a KA-6D tanker provided another camera position, plus a means to stretching filming time by refuelling the fighters.

The growing age of reconnaissance aircraft such as the RF-8 Crusader and the RA-5C Vigilante and the low performance of their on-board sensors forced the USN to consider an interim recce system which could serve until the planned RF-18 Hornet became available. The solution was to develop the Tactical Air Reconnaissance Pod System (TARPS), a lightweight add-on unit which could be carried by the F-14. Carried on one of the F-14's Phoenix missile stations, it imposes little penalty in aircraft performance or flight characteristics, and does not interfere with the carriage and launch of missiles. TARPS may easily be removed when no longer required. Within half an hour the aircraft can be restored to normal fighter status.

Development started in April 1976, and work on interfacing it with the F-14 was under way by September. The specification was demanding. According to Lt Cdr James Flaherty, operations officer for VF-84, 'Back in 74–75 we weren't sure such an externally mounted pod could produce a quality photo product.' Flight testing by the USN began in September 1977, and led to a limited production go-ahead a year later. Approval for service use was given in May 1979, allowing full-rate production to begin. This was completed in FY84.

TARPS is 17 ft (5.2 m) long and weighs 1750 lb (794 kg). It contains a KS-87B forward/vertical oblique film camera, a KA-99 horizon-to-horizon panoramic film camera, an AAD-5A imaging infrared sensor, plus associated support equipment including the data display set used to provide control signals and data annotation to the sensors, a control indicator power distribution unit (CIPDU) which contains diagnostic consoles, plus an environmental control system for equipment cooling and window de-fogging.

The pod makes few demands on the parent aircraft, only power, signal and air-conditioning connections. It is controlled via the Controller Processor Signal, a small panel located on the RIO's left-hand console. Data from the pod is displayed on the cockpit-mounted TID display, showing information such as range and time to target, range and time to the CAMERA OFF command, pod status, and IR scanner field of view. Symbology projected onto the HUD includes target position, the command ground track line, and a steering cue.

TARPS was deployed for the first time in the second half of 1981, entering service on the US east coast with VF-84 aboard *Nimitz*, then on the west coast with VF-211 aboard *Constellation*. Four crews from each squadron were given formal TARPS training, later passing their expertize on to other squadron aircrew so that all would be able to fly recce missions as required. Normally three of a squadron's 12 aircraft would be TARPS-equipped. During the first four months of deployment, VF-84 flew more than 100 reconnaissance missions, with a 92 per cent success rate. With the retirement of the last RF-8G in the spring of 1982, the TARPS-equipped F-14 became the Navy's main tactical reconnaissance system.

One task assigned to the new equipment was the photography of Soviet long-range surveillance aircraft, a project intended to catalogue the different equipment configurations installed on these snooping monitors. It is possible that TARPS-equipped F-14s have been used in Central America. In September 1983 Cuba claimed that USAF RC-135 reconnaissance aircraft had flown 33 stories into Nicaraguan airspace in the previous three months, and that more than 100 other flights had been noted by aircraft ranging from the F-14, Dassault Super Mystere, and Cessna A-37 to transports, light aircraft and helicopters.

When TARPS was first developed, it was intended to be interim equipment to fill the gap between the phasing out of older recce equipment and the arrival of a new, dedicated recce platform. It will eventually be replaced by the planned RF-18, which will carry a variant of TARPS known as TARS (Tactical Air Reconnaissance System). TARS will be installed in the nose of the F-18, but its sensors will still be replaceable. Currently in advanced development, TARS first flew in an F-18 in August 1984. The USN would like to deploy 124 RF-18 fighters, replacing elderly aircraft such as RF-4Bs still operated by USN and Marine units, but the new aircraft is not due to be ordered into production until the late 1980s to meet a FY89 target date for deployment. As a result, TARPS is now likely to remain in front-line service for at least a decade.

Chapter 4
Tomcat shows its teeth

In the six years which followed Tomcat's brief forays over South Vietnam, the aircraft led a generally uneventful existence—a story of routine deployments and training exercises. When the carriers *Forrestal* and *Nimitz* moved into the Gulf of Sidra in the southern Mediterranean in mid-August 1981, Tomcat was to carry out what should have been another routine training exercise—practice missile shoots.

The exercise was taking place in waters over which Libya claimed territorial rights, so no-one was surprised when on the first day of the exercise—18 August—Libyan aircraft came out to monitor the operation. Approaching in pairs, the Libyan fighters were intercepted by Tomcats from the carriers. Some flights took little action as the F-14s approached, while others attempted to manoeuvre into offensive positions. No shots were fired by either side, but by the end of the day more than 30 two-aircraft sections had been intercepted. Several types of aircraft were involved—Mirages, MiG-23 *Floggers*, Su-22 *Fitters* and the pride of Libya's Air Force, the MiG-25 *Foxbat*.

The next day, Tomcats again took position on CAP (Combat Air Patrol) duty, and the pattern of the previous day's activities seemed to be repeating itself. At 7.15 am, and towards the end of their CAP, a pair of VF-41 Tomcats—107 flown by VF-41 commanding officer Cdr Henry Kleemann and NFO Lt Dave Venlet, and 112 flown by Lt Larry Muczynski and NFO Lt Steve Walker—detected two fighters taking off from a Libyan airbase which they had been watching using the AWG-9's long-range capability.

The Libyan aircraft climbed to match the 22,000 ft (6700 m) operating height of the Tomcats, then flew straight towards the two USN aircraft. Attempts to out-manoeuvre the approaching aircraft failed, thanks to good work by the Libyan GCI (Ground Control Intercept) station which was monitoring the

incident, so at 10 miles range the Tomcats positioned themselves for a head-on approach. Muczynski and Walker in 112 deliberately positioned themselves 6000–8000 ft (1800–2400 m) above Kleemann and Venlet in 107, while the latter attempted to close the range and get visual identification. At a range of around eight miles, Kleeman visually located the Libyan aircraft.

As the distance closed to around 1000 ft (300 m), 112 began to turn in order to fly over the intruders—now identified as Su-22 *Fitters*. As 107 manoeuvred into a similar turn, Muczynski saw a missile leave the port side of one of the leading Libyan aircraft. He called a warning to 112, but noted almost immediately that the missile had failed to guide correctly.

The rules of engagement specified that the Tomcats could open fire if fired upon, so both Tomcats headed for the Libyan lead aircraft. The two Sukhois had split up after missile launch, and the leader was now in a climbing left-hand turn. Realizing that 120 was well positioned to deal with the leader, 107 broke off, turning instead to get into

OPPOSITE TOP
Sukhoi Su-22 Fitter J *of the Libyan Air Force. A day after this photograph was taken, two similar aircraft attempted to engage two US Navy F-14s from VF-41 'Black Aces'.* Fitter J *is a remarkable example of the ability of Soviet engineers to extract the maximum usefulness from an elderly basic design, but the aircraft and its AA-2* Atoll *heat-seeking missiles were no match for* Tomcat. *Both Libyan aircraft were shot down in the ensuing dogfight*
(US Navy)

OPPOSITE BOTTOM
Sukhoi killer: Tomcat of VF-41 'Black Aces', side number 107, buno 160390, was the second of the two aircraft which downed Libyan Fitters. *This photo was taken at NAS Oceana on 4 April 1982*
(Robert F Dorr)

Flight deck operations on Nimitz: a Tomcat of VF-41 taxies to the catapult. A KA-6D Intruder tanker is positioned on the other waist catapult (Jean-Pierre Montbazet)

position on the tail of the other Libyan aircraft, which was by now heading into the sun but turning. As soon as the Libyan wingman's turn had reached the point where the sunlight would not interfere with a Sidewinder shot, 107 fired an AIM-9L from its left glove hardpoint. Range was about a quarter of a mile (1.2 km) and the round homed on the *Fitter*, striking it in the tail. The Sukhoi rolled, the drag chute deployed, and five seconds after missile impact the Libyan pilot ejected.

By now the Libyan leader had completed his climbing turn, but 112 was in position for a tail shot—another AIM-9L—once again from the port glove. Range was half a mile (0.8 km) and the round guided perfectly, flying up the tailpipe of the Su-22's Lyulka engine. The resulting explosion blew the tail section off the *Fitter*, sending the Libyan fighter into a spin. The pilot ejected, but no parachute was seen. The brief air battle—the first to be fought between VG fighters—had lasted less than a minute.

The Soviet view of the dogfight, as given by Moscow Radio, was predictably colourful. In a broadcast of February 1982 which described recent operations by the carrier *Nimitz*, listeners were told how '... American F-14 fighters attacked and shot down two Libyan patrol planes. Having carried out this bandit-like raid, the vultures returned to their floating base.' The title of the broadcast 'The Atomic-Powered Pirate' gave some indication of the

impression which the performance of the carrier and its Tomcats made on the Soviet Government.

On 6 June 1982, Israel launched 'Operation Peace for Galilee'—the invasion of Lebanon. Publicly, the announced goal was to clear the forces of the Palestine Liberation Organization (PLO) from a 25 mile (40 km) strip of south Lebanon in order to end cross-border raids and bombardment of Israeli settlements, but high on the Israeli priority list was the desire to expel the PLO from Lebanon. One unforeseen result was to be a combat deployment for Tomcat.

As the Israeli Air Force fought against Syrian MiGs and surface-to-air missile sites in the Bekka Valley area, the ground forces swept north with more than 30,000 men, capturing PLO strongholds at Beaufort Castle and Nabatiyeh, seized the port cities of Tyre, Sidon and Damour, and laid siege to West Beirut. Israeli infantry and armoured units clashed with their Syrian opposite numbers in the hills east of Beirut, gaining control over the road to Damascus and preventing Syrian reinforcements from reaching the city.

The ten-week siege of West Beirut was the sort of warfare for which the Israel Defence Forces were ill-prepared. Earlier in the same year, British units had

Two aircraft of VF-41 rendezvous with one of Nimitz'
KA-6D tankers
(Grumman)

captured Port Stanley from its Argentinian defenders with the loss of only a handful of civilian lives, but the Israeli attack on Beirut showed no such skill, and was largely a matter of battering the defenders with heavy artillery. In mid-August the PLO agreed to leave Beirut. Abandoning their heavy equipment, they left Lebanon, travelling to Algeria, Iraq, Jordan, Sudan, Syria, Tunisia, and North and South Yemen. The evacuation was supervised by a multi-national force made up of US, French and Italian troops, which were soon withdrawn once the PLO had gone.

On 10 September, as the multinational force began to withdraw from Lebanon, its task apparently completed, President Gemayel of Lebanon was killed in an explosion in East Beirut. Israel occupied East Beirut on the 15th, and a massacre of Palestinians in the Sabra and Shantila camps by Lebanese Pahalangist troops operating under nominal Israeli control followed on 16 to 18 September. On the 19th, Israel began to withdraw from Beirut, and the multi-national force returned the next day.

An increase in the size of the 4,100-strong force was requested by the Lebanese Government on 29 November. Hopes that the force would be allowed to carry out its mission were dented on 15 March when US and Italian soldiers were wounded. On 18 April, a terrorist group known as Islamic Jihad ('Holy War') bombed the US Embassy in Beirut, killing 47 people. It was obvious that the Lebanese Government and

Army were too weak to control the situation, and that Lebanon's long-running civil war was about to move into a new and dangerous phase.

Fighting between guerilla factions broke out on 4 June. By 2 August, this involved heavy fighting between Druze and Christian militia in the Chouf mountains near Beirut. Street fighting killed two US Marines and three French soldiers on 29 August. On 4 September, the Israeli forces started to withdraw to new positions along the Alawi river. As they retreated, the Christian militia attempted to move into the area, and fighting began between them, the Druze, and the Lebanese Army.

President Reagan ordered a US amphibious group to back up the forces in Lebanon. On 7 September the Lebanese Government requested help in dealing with the fighting in the Chouf mountains, and the next day US warships began to fire on Druze positions, supporting government troops attempting to defend the town of Suq al-Gharb.

On 9 September, Tomcats from the carrier *Eisenhower* overflew Beirut on reconnaissance missions. On the 11th, a Marine Corps spokesman confirmed that Tomcats from *Eisenhower* were flying 'tactical reconnaissance missions' in support of the

153

OPPOSITE TOP
A VF-41 Tomcat, side number 110, successfully engages one of the four arrestor wires strung across the deck of Nimitz
(Jean-Pierre Montbazet)

OPPOSITE BOTTOM
This view of a VF-41 Tomcat clearly shows the chin-mounted antenna of the ALQ-100 jamming suite, and the shape of the fairing used to streamline belly-mounted Phoenix missiles
(Grumman)

ABOVE
Tomcat goes in harm's way—this photo of a VF-143 'The World Famous Pukin' Dogs' aircraft over the Chouf Mountains in Lebanon was taken by its TARPS-equipped flight companion. Syrian attacks on recce Tomcats operating over Lebanon led to a US Navy air strike
(US Navy, VF-143)

US Navy and Marines, and that missions had been flown over the Chouf and Aley mountains. Alleging US 'creeping aggression' the Soviet Union claimed on 14 September that the Tomcats flying over Lebanon were armed for 'striking ground targets.'

During the night of 18 to 19 September, the US contingent stationed on the perimeter of Beirut International Airport exchanged light weapons fire with gunmen throughout the night. At 1030 on the 19th, USN Tomcats from *Eisenhower* flew reconnaissance sorties over Beirut, but a US Navy spokesman denied reports that they had pursued Syrian MiGs over central Lebanon.

F-14s flew over Beirut at 0030 on 21 September, and later the same day French Etendard fighters bombed positions in the mountains around Beirut. Two days later F-14s from *Eisenhower* overflew Lebanon's central mountains at about the same time that Syrian MiGs flew over the Bekaa Valley in eastern Lebanon, raising the possibility that the two air arms might clash.

Tension continued to rise following the suicide truck attacks on 23 October which killed 239 US Marines and 58 French paratroopers. The technique was repeated on 4 November, when another suicide bomber destroyed the Israeli Army's headquarters in Tyre, killing 60 people.

On 10 November, Syria reported that its Lebanon-based air defence units had clashed for the first time with US aircraft. 'Four enemy planes flew over our positions in Lebanon at 0530 GMT. Our air defence system confronted them and forced them to return toward the sea.' Syria's state radio later identified the aircraft involved as Tomcats. The aircraft—which were on a reconnaissance sortie from the *Eisenhower* flew over Beirut and the central mountains, came under attack when Syrian positions fired surface-to-air missiles.

US Defense Secretary Caspar W Weinberger appeared to play down the incident at first, telling a group of foreign journalists in Washington, 'Our

An Egyptian Air Force F-4E Phantom leads a novel formation during exercise 'Bright Star' in 1983. Gathered around an F-14A Tomcat are (clockwise from the top) a MiG-21, F-16, F-4, Mirage 5, Shenyang F-6, A-6 Intruder, MiG-17 and an A-7 Corsair (US Navy)

information is that we had normal reconnaissance flights with normal results in the Beirut area.' Weinberger said such flights are 'standard practice.' 'There is nothing unusual or different going on,' he said. He later remarked that 'I don't regard it unusual or surprising' that the Tomcats had been fired on, but stated that 'we don't know that the Syrians fired' at the F-14s, which were operating from the aircraft carrier *Eisenhower* off Lebanon.

Syria called up army reserves and ordered a general military mobilization. Israel staged a mobilization drill to test its own war readiness, but assured Syria that no attack against them was planned. US newspaper and television reports suggesting that President Reagan was contemplating a retaliatory strike in response to the 23 October bombing contributed to the tension, but the US Government also insisted that it had no plans to attack Syria and urged Damascus to show 'restraint and prudence.'

Formations of Tomcats from *Eisenhower* made repeated runs over Beirut and the surrounding mountains before midnight on 13 November and at dawn. On 17 November a French air raid was launched on Lebanese Shi'ite bases in the Bekaa Valley in retaliation for the 23 October bombing of French troops.

On 23 November, F-14 and A-7 aircraft from the carrier *Independence* flew patrols over Beirut. Three days later, a US spokesman identified aircraft reported over the Lebanon as F-14 Tomcats flying 'over areas under the control of our forces in Lebanon.' An F-14 overflight of Syrian positions was reported that day, with Syria claiming that 'our air

defences confronted them and forced them to return seaward.'

In other incidents, US reconnaissance aircraft were repeatedly being fired upon, and matters came to a crisis on 3 December when two Tomcats were attacked by what a Pentagon spokesman described as 'a heavy volume of anti-aircraft fire and at least 10 surface-to-air missiles.' Reagan decided to act, ordering a bombing attack the next day against Syrian-controlled mountains 23 miles (30 km) east of Beirut. Tomcats were reported flying top cover for the strike formation, but no fighter opposition was reported as A-6 Intruder and A-7 Corsair II attack aircraft struck Syrian gun batteries at about 8 am.

Two aircraft were shot down—an A-6 and an A-7—apparently by SA-7 man-portable SAMs. The A-7 crashed into a residential area in Jounieh, on the Lebanese coast, and the pilot parachuted into the Mediterranean and was rescued. The A-6 crashed into a barren mountainside near Kfar Salwan, 15 miles (24 km) east of Beirut. The Intruder crew were captured, but one—badly injured in the crash—died a few hours later.

A Pentagon spokesman confirmed that the air strikes were in retaliation for Syria's attempt to down the Tomcats the day before. 'The Syrian authorities clearly knew they were firing on US reconnaissance aircraft and the volume of fire makes it clear that it was not locally directed or random.'

Twelve hours after the raid, the US Marine encampment at Beirut International Airport came under heavy artillery, rocket, and small-arms fire, which killed eight men and injured two more. The deaths brought the number of American servicemen killed in Lebanon since the Marines arrived in September 1982 to 254. The barrage lasted for around four and a half hours, and the Marines fired back with small arms, heavy machine guns, automatic weapons, M-60 tanks, and 155 mm artillery. US Navy vessels operating offshore provided fire support.

On 6 December, ten F-14s flew over Beirut at mid-afternoon and headed in the direction of the upper Metn mountains, apparently on a reconnaissance mission. On the same day, US Navy Admiral Stansfield Turner—director of the US Central Intelligence Agency during the Carter administration—criticized the use of Tomcats as reconnaissance aircraft. 'If we wanted photos of Lebanon, we could have done it with total safety' he told the National Commission on Free and Responsible Media, a citizen's group affiliated with the US Chamber of Commerce. Instead of relying on the proven capability of the Lockheed SR-71, '... we go fly around up there and wait until they shoot at us.' The F-14 patrols were dismissed as '... a threat, a demonstration, a political gesture.'

On 13 December, anti-aircraft missiles were again fired at Tomcats on reconnaissance flights over the upper Metn Mountains. In this case the retaliation was swift. Soon after the aircrew radioed back that they were under attack, US Navy warships began a bombardment of Syrian positions, and repeated the shelling the following day.

On 18 December two US F-14 aircraft from the carrier *Independence* overflew Syrian positions while on a reconnaissance mission, and were engaged by air defence units. Immediately after the aircraft had flown back out to sea, two US warships anchored west of Juniyah opened fire on Syrian units in the area for a period of 15 minutes. 'As a result of this aggression, one military vehicle was hit,' a Syrian military spokesman later claimed.

The reconnaissance sorties continued at almost daily intervals, and by the end of the year anti-SAM countermeasures were apparently in operation. On 31 December, journalists covering the conflict reported that two Tomcats from the *Independence* had released 'heat balloons to deflect ground-to-air missiles' while flying at low level towards the Syrian-controlled area of central Lebanon.

Within minutes of a surface-to-air missile being fired at an American helicopter over the US Marine base at Beirut International Airport on 28 January, F-14s were launched to fly sweeps over the southern suburbs of Beirut and the neighbouring hills. Similar sweeps were flown later that day by USN F-4 Phantoms, but neither operation drew ground fire, and no ordnance was dropped.

On 9 February, another clash between the US Navy and the Syrian Air Force was reported. A Syrian military spokesman in Damascus reported that 'the American Navy continued escalating the military situation and bombarded positions of the Lebanese national movement in the Chouf and Sofar. US F-14s also attacked, and our air defences confronted them and forced them fly back westwards.' The naval bombardment was apparently a retaliation for the shelling of east Beirut.

Open conflict between the Tomcats and Syrian MiGs was avoided. As the situation became more chaotic, the futility of Western peacekeeping efforts became obvious and their forces were withdrawn from Lebanon. In April and May of the following year, the Israeli Army was to follow suit.

Events in Lebanon may have dominated the headlines, but throughout the period, carrier based F-14s had formed part of the US military presence in other parts of the world. Back in April 1983 two USN Tomcats from the carrier *America* were fired on by Somali troops while overflying the Somali port of Berbera on the Gulf of Aden, but in this case no military reaction or retaliation was necessary. The F-14s were on a pre-arranged photo-reconnaissance mission, but the Somali Defence Ministry had apparently forgotten to inform army units in Berbera. Mistaking the US fighters for Ethiopian attackers, the ground forces opened fire with anti-aircraft guns and, according to some reports, launched a surface-to-air missile. No damage or injury was caused, and the aircraft returned safely to the carrier.

Joint Egyptian/US/UK exercises held in the autumn of 1983 saw the Tomcat pitted once more against Soviet-designed fighters. After the manoeuvres, Air Marshal Hilmi reported that an Egyptian Air Force MiG-19 had managed to intercept a USN Tomcat, preventing it from reaching its target. Egypt pronounced itself satisfied with the results of the joint exercises. According to Hilmi, the EAF had been able to benefit from the dogfight experience gained by Britain during the Falklands conflict.

In the summer of 1984, Tomcats returned to the Gulf of Sidra and the news headlines when the US DoD announced that F-14s had overflown the disputed area on 25 July without giving advance public notice. Libya duly termed the overflights 'blatant aggression' and promised to defend the area 'at whatever cost'. Announcing that the US intrusion had involved 164 Tomcats, the JANA newsagency claimed that Libyan fighters had driven off some of the US aircraft. Libya announced military manoeuvres using live ammunition, and public demonstrations protested against this 'provocation', but the incident ended quietly.

Chapter 5
Revolution and War

'In the name of God, the Merciful, the Compassionate. At 0945 today, in a dogfight between our daring fighter aircraft and the frustrated enemy aircraft, one enemy F-14 aircraft was shot down over Khafajiyah (Susangerd) inside enemy territory. All our fighter aircraft returned safely to base, praise be to God.'

The style of the announcement may be quaint by Western standards, but the story it told is a simple one—confirmation that Grumman's swing-wing warplane was involved in a war. Thousands of miles from the Calverton production line where they first took shape, Tomcats were in action in the hands of the only export customer ever to order the type, the Iranian Air Force.

Iran, formerly Persia, was for many years totally under the influence of the West. When the Shah first ascended the throne in 1941 after a British-engineered coup which had toppled his father, he was widely seen as little more than a puppet controlled by the Anglo-Iranian Oil Company (later to become BP). With the coming to power of Dr Mossedeq in 1951, Anglo-Iranian was nationalized. The Shah was eventually exiled by the new leader, only to be returned to the throne in 1953 after a coup organized by the CIA and the British secret service.

During the 1950s and early 1960s the Iranian armed forces were dependent on US and British military aid. In the early 1960s, the Imperial Iranian Air Force (IIAF) was little more than a token force numbering around 140 aircraft of all types. Its front-line fighter was the veteran F-86 Sabre.

The 1960s saw the Shah invest his oil revenues in modernizing his armed forces, and the IIAF was transformed into a well-equipped air arm. In 1962 Northrop F-5A and B Freedom Fighters were purchased to replace the ageing Sabres, and in 1966 an order was placed for the F-4D Phantom. The IIAF was now in a privileged position. Until then,

only the UK had been permitted to buy the McDonnell Douglas warplane. A total of 32 were delivered between 1968 and 1969.

Since World War 2 the United Kingdom had maintained a military presence in the area, but this policy was to fall victim of repeated defence cuts

Grumman's twin-tailed Tomcat emblem developed an oriental look in this first draft of a commemorative decal, but the design was never used. The IIAF apparently considered this 'Arabian Nights' image unsatisfactory. The design finally approved for release is reproduced on the back cover of this book

Aircraft 3-863, the first destined for Iran, lifts off from Calverton Field on 5 December 1975 (Grumman)

made by the Labour Government which came to power in 1964. With around 27 per cent of the defence budget being spent on overseas deployments, and the value of Sterling dropping, cuts in overseas forces were too attractive to resist. Rather than attempting to maintain a reduced presence, plus base facilities which would allow emergency re-inforcement of the region, the Wilson Government decided to withdraw all forces from the area by 1971. Despite the election of a Conservative Government in 1970, no attempt was made to reverse the decision. British forces pulled out of the area in 1971 as planned, leaving a power vacuum into which the Shah was determined to step. Even before the last British forces had left the region, Iran occupied several islands in the Gulf.

Iran proved a valuable market for the arms industries of the USA and UK. Most weaponry came from the USA, which supplied arms worth $17 billion between 1970 and 1979, but the UK picked-up valuable orders for Chieftain and Shir main battle tanks, Rapier SAMs, and various logistic ships. In 1978 alone, the US sold weaponry worth $358.4 million, while deliveries exceeded $1.9 billion in value. During 1979 FMS deliveries totalled an astounding $2.4 billion.

The F-5As were replaced in the early 1970s by the Northrop F-5E. Under the Peace Rush programme, 141 were ordered under a contract worth $377 million, and the total number taken into service was eventually to rise to 309. The F-4D fleet was soon supplemented by a massive order for the F-4E.

Under the Peace Guard, Peace Roll and Peace Roll II programmes, 177 were delivered between 1971 and 1977. Cost to Iran was $857 million. To provide a reconnaissance capability, 16 RF-4Es were purchased. Four were delivered between 1968–69, four more in 1971, and the final eight between 1976 and 1977. Six Lockheed P-3F Orion maritime-patrol aircraft were also delivered under a $37 million contract.

In May 1972, President Nixon visited Iran, and the Shah raised a delicate issue—the Soviet MiG-25 *Foxbat*. For some time, the Soviet Air Force had been flying reconnaissance missions over Iranian territory and the IIAF's current equipment lacked the performance to deal with intruders which flew at Mach 2.5 or more. Nixon proved sympathetic, telling the Shah that he could order the F-14 Tomcat or F-15 Eagle, and would receive the necessary technical support to operate the aircraft.

Grumman lost no time in pointing out to the US Navy that an Iranian F-14 order could reduce the unit cost of the aircraft, and spent $250,000 promoting the aircraft at the 1973 Paris *Salon*. To lobby for Tomcat, Grumman hired Houshang Lavi, a brother-in-law of the Shah and a close friend of Iranian Air Force Commander General Khatami. In August 1973 the Shah selected the F-14, and the sale was approved by the US Government in November 1973. The initial order signed in January 1974 covered 30 Tomcats, but in June of that year, a further 50 were ordered.

Before the aircraft were delivered, several problems were to arise. In the autumn of 1974, Iran's government-owned Melli Bank had to provide Grumman with a $75 million loan to ensure the future of the F-14 programme. In the following spring, the Iranian Government learned that Lavi had been acting as a Grumman agent, and that payments of $28 million had been made by Grumman. Iranian Minister for War, General Toufanian, told a Press conference that, 'This shows that the foreign companies want to loot us. We will not allow this,' and he insisted that the money be repaid to Iran.

The build standard of Iran's Tomcats was virtually identical to that of the US Navy version. Only a few

items of highly-classified avionics are not installed. Having studied the US Navy's Tomcat training facilities at NAS Miramar, the IIAF decided to create an Iranian equivalent.

Base site for Iranian Tomcat operations was at Isfahan. On a flat plateau 20 miles southeast of the city a new air base was created, complete with two 14,000 ft runways, a control tower, hardened aircraft shelters, and housing for personnel. Grumman staff would be based here, and at avionics and airframe depots at Mehrabad. IIAF aircrew began to arrive in the USA for training in May 1974, and soon afterwards the first Grumman pilots went to Iran to study IIAF operating procedures, and to begin in-country aircrew training.

The first of 80 Tomcats was delivered to the IIAF in January 1976, flying from the USA via Spain. By this time Grumman's in-country support programme involved large numbers of expatriates—800

(including their families) were now stationed in Iran. Iran's massive arms purchases had resulted in large numbers of foreign technicians being resident in Iran, visible evidence to the populace of Iran's military dependence on outsiders. The assassination in August 1976 of three Rockwell executives in Teheran gave warning of just how volatile Iran was beneath the veneer of outward stability.

Transition onto the F-14 was slow initially, largely a result of a stretchout in the construction schedule for ground facilities. By May 1977 when Iran celebrated the 50th anniversary of the Royal House, 21 had been delivered, all but one of which took part in an air display. The MiG-25s were still risking overflights—in the summer of that year, one *Foxbat* crossing the country at 65,000 ft (19,814 m) and flying at Mach 2 was tracked by the radar of an IIAF F-14. The Shah decided to act, and ordered that live firing tests of Phoenix be carried out. In August IIAF crews

downed a BQM-34E drone flying at 50,000 ft (16,150 m) and another at 500 ft (150 m). MiG-25 overflights promptly ended. Tomcat deliveries were completed in 1978, with the delivery of the 79th aircraft. One IIAF Tomcat remained in the USA in order to act as a testbed for modifications.

By the time that the final Tomcats were being delivered, it was clear that the Shah was facing significant internal unrest. Political repression, unemployment, a widening gap between the standard of living of the rich and poor, a reaction against Western-style materialism, and an upsurge in Islamic fundamentalism all combined to create a situation which was soon out of control. In 1978 alone, at least 2,000 Iranians were killed in riots. The unrest started in the city of Qom, a religious centre, in January of that year, but it spread rapidly.

Martial law failed to contain the problem, and a short-lived military government under General Gholam Reza Azhari tried unsuccessfully to stabilize the country. A civilian government led by the Shah's long-standing opponent Shahpour Bakhtiar was unable to win popular support, and the Shah, his health undermined by disease, left the country on 16 January. On 1 February, the charismatic religious leader Ayatollah Khomenei returned to Iran after a 16 year exile, triggering off a chaotic period which was to result in the proclamation of an Islamic republic on 1 April 1979.

The resulting changes in Iran's political, social and economic life were widespread, as the country fell into the grip of Islamic fundamentalism and rejected both Western and communist lifestyles. Following the revolution, the new government embarked on a massive series of cancellations. This saw the US lose orders worth more than $9 billion, and the British Royal Ordnance Factory tank plant virtually denuded of work. Cancellations affecting the Iranian Air Force included:

60 General Dynamics F-16 Fighting Falcons

7 Boeing E-3A Sentry Airborne Warning and Control System aircraft

16 McDonnell Douglas RF-4E reconnaissance aircraft

400 AIM-54A Phoenix missiles

200 McDonnell Douglas Harpoon anti-ship missiles

Other programmes were allowed to continue. Foreign Military Sales deliveries to Iran in FY79

Tomcats on the flight line at Isfahan. By the time that this photo was taken, aircrew and technicians were coping with their new mount, albeit with large-scale assistance by Grumman. With the Iranian Revolution and the withdrawal of US support, intelligence sources predicted that these aircraft would soon be non-operational. In the short term, they probably were, but Iran now has a substantial number of Tomcats flying (Grumman)

amounted to $2.4 billion while commercial sales accounted for a further $109 million. The reprieve was to be short-lived.

Events of the next few years were to see Iran break with both superpowers. Relations with the USA were soured by the occupation of the US embassy in Teheran by militant students who held 52 Americans hostage for more than a year. Although the hostages were released in early 1981, the US cut all political and military ties with Iran, imposing a strict arms embargo. Military equipment worth around $300 million and scheduled for delivery to Iran was immediately impounded. This decision had a severe long-term effect on the Tomcat fleet, since more than half of the 'frozen' orders covered F-14 spares. The single US-based Iranian Tomcat was never delivered, but placed in storage.

Deliveries of military equipment to Iran ceased by the end of 1979, and in April 1980, President Carter decided that the impounded equipment 'be made available for use by the US military forces or for sale to other countries'. New US restrictions announced in September 1984 prohibit the export of virtually all patterns of aircraft and equipment which could be converted from civil to military use. This covers light aircraft, small helicopters and even marine outboard motors.

The Soviet Union was an early supporter of the Khomeini regime. It praised Khomeini's split with the USA, supported Iran during the hostage crisis, and offered military, technical and economic assistance. These policies failed to defend the Soviet state from the wrath of the mullahs. The Soviet Union was attacked as 'godless', and Iran lent assistance to the

Iranian Tomcats were finished in the standard brown and green camouflage finish of the Imperial Iranian Air Force (IIAF)
(Grumman)

rebels in Afghanistan, expelled 18 Soviet diplomats and jailed more than 1,000 members of Tudeh, the Iranian communist party.

Relations with the rest of the Islamic world have not been much smoother, largely a result of three factors. Iran is not part of the Arab world, and the traditional tendency of Iranians to regard themselves as superior to their Arab neighbours has not been helpful. Iran adheres to the Shi'ite sect, while the majority of the world's Muslims belong to the Sunni sect. A final factor has been the Khomeini regime's zealous desire to promote its own brand of fundamentalist beliefs throughout the Middle East. Iran therefore found itself with few friends in the Islamic world, receiving support only from Libya and Syria.

Armed clashes between Iran and Iraq started in May 1979. The sources of friction between the two countries are complex, and include disagreements over a the disputed Shatt-el-Arab waterway, hostility due to Iranian support for the Kurdish rebellion in northern Iraq, and Iran's occupation of the islands of Abu Musa and Tumb in the approaches to the Strait of Homuz, plus the desire to recover territory ceded to Iran by a 1975 treaty. Less prominent was the threat posed to Iraqi society by Islamic fundamentalism. Established as a Hashemite kingdom under British Mandate following World War 1, Iraq became a socialist state after a coup in 1958 which deposed King Faisal II. The population is 55 per cent Shi'ite Moslem, 40 per cent Sunni Moslem and 5 per cent Christian, a combination which could be rendered unstable by any importation of Khomeini-style Shi'ite fundamentalism, particularly amongst the Kurds.

War with Iraq finally broke out in September 1980. On the 17th, Iraq cancelled the 1975 border treaty, and three days later, Iran mobilized its reserve forces. On the 22nd, Iraq went to war, opening the campaign with an attempted pre-emptive strike on Iranian air bases, and a three-pronged ground attack over the disputed border. The war soon settled into a military stalemate in which each side seemed to lack the ability to achieve a decisive breakthrough.

Despite the lack of spares for its US weaponry and alternative sources of high-tech war *matériel*, Iran has been holding its own against better-equipped Iraqi forces. It successfully defended Khorramshahr and Susangerd, and counter-attacked against the Iraqi invaders, driving them back into their own territory. A stubborn Iraqi defence, which included the use of chemical warfare, prevented any major Iranian advances, and the war settled into what at times looked like a re-run of the Battle of the Somme.

A weakened Iranian Air Force—now known as the Islamic Republic of Iran Air Force (IRIAF)—found itself in action against a foe which if not fully combat experienced, had at least seen some action against Israel. In the heavy fighting which marked the opening stages of the war, and the repeated flare-ups which have continued to the present day, Iran has suffered heavy losses in personnel and in equipment such as aircraft, helicopters, warships and tanks.

Despite this bloodletting, the Iranian air force has been able to continue operations, causing Iraq to request better aircraft from its suppliers. Iraqi Su-22 *Fitter* strike aircraft operating on strike missions into Iranian airspace were repeatedly intercepted by Iranian Air Force F-4 Phantoms until the Iraqis adopted a policy of escorting its strike formations with Mirage F.1 fighters equipped with jamming pods. The latter are probably fitted with Thomson-CSF jamming pods—either the *Remora* jammer (designed for self-protection) or the more powerful *Caiman* offensive jammer.

Despite the existence of Tupolev Tu-16 and Tu-22 bombers at the start of the war, and the subsequent delivery of Mirage F.1 and MiG-25 *Foxbat* fighters, plus Super Etendard strike aircraft, as well as missiles to arm these new types, Iran was still winning the air war. If Iraq continued its recent air strikes beyond the immediate battlefield areas, Iran might and could penetrate into Iraqi territory and attack similar targets.

Commander-in-chief of the Iranian armed forced is the President, who also leads the seven-man Supreme Defence Council made up of the President, Prime Minister, Defence Minister, Chief of Staff, the head of the Revolutionary Guards, and two further members directly appointed by Ayatollah Khomeini.

Prior to the revolution, 413,000 men were in uniform. The current total is said to be around two million, including some 250,000 serving in para-military forces such as the gendarmerie, the Basij, and the Revolutionary Guards. The latter—known as the Pasdaran—could eventually replace Iran's regular army. Made up of Islamic zealots, the force includes large numbers of young Iranians who have offered to become martyrs. The Basij Popular Mobilization Force is less well organized, but has seen action in the war against Iraq.

Since the war began, Iran's military budget has been maintained at around 300,000 million rials (c. $4,000 million), falling briefly to 210,000 million rials ($3,000 million) in 1981. The cost is now escalating. In January 1984 Iranian Prime Minister Hussein Moussavi gave the cost of the war at almost $11 million a day, but announced that this could be increased to $16 million a day if necessary.

Despite the strains of revolution and war, the country still has considerable economic clout, thanks to its rising oil revenues. Despite the humiliation of the year-long captivity of its diplomats in 1979–80, even the USA still buys Iranian petroleum products, with imports from this source accounting for around 1.5 per cent of total US consumption. Iran has the capability to choke the Straits of Hormuz, through which passes nearly 47 per cent of the oil that feeds both the US and the Western industrialized nations.

The current Iranian national budget is around $40 billion, of which the current military budget accounts for only some 10 per cent. Although $4 billion has been allocated for military spending in FY84, Iranian Prime Minister Mir-Hossein Moussavi told Parliament in November 1983 that if the situation warranted, he would increase the country's military budget to $5.7 billion.

This move to less formal military forces such as the Revolutionary Guards has had little effect on the Islamic Republic of Iran Air Force, which currently numbers around 35,000 men. Major bases are located at Teheran, Hamadan, Dexful, Doshen-Tappeh, Mehrabab, Galeh-Marghi, Zahidan, Masbad, Shiraz, Ahwaz, Isfahan, Tabriz, Faharabad and Chah Bahar.

Accurate information on the current state of the IRIAF is near-impossible to obtain, although some evidence can be gleaned from combat reports, propaganda claims of both sides, and information 'leaked' from Western intelligence services. Iran has reportedly lost more than 100 of its F-4s and F-5s. Additionally, its fighters, helicopters and tanks are said to be unserviceable for lack of spares and maintenance. According to Western military analysts, Iran now probably deploys about 90 aircraft, of which 60–70 may be combat types. Main combat elements are the F-4 and F-5. By mid-1985, attrition and lack of spares had reduced the operational fleet to about 30–36 F-4s, three RF-4Es, and 17–21 F-5s.

These aircraft operated mainly from Shiraz, Bushehr and Bandar Abbas. Five of the six P-3Fs are still operational, although the serviceability of their avionics is not known. Several were reported to be tracking shipping in the Persian Gulf in June 1984.

Iran had ordered 714 Phoenix missiles, but only 284 had been delivered at the time of the Revolution. Delivery of a further 150 which had been accepted from the manufacturer but not yet shipped from the USA, fell victim to the US embargo, and the final 90 rounds ordered by Iran were never built. No detailed figures of AIM-7 Sparrow deliveries are available, but stocks of AIM-9 Sidewinder missiles were healthier—a total of 768 had been delivered between 1968–71.

Until the summer of 1984 it was believed that Iran lacked the technical ability and the spare parts to get the F-14s into the air. The common Western view was that expressed by Pentagon sources, which claimed that most of the F-14s were unserviceable. Only some four or five were maintained in flying

condition, largely by a process of cannibalization. Current role of these survivors was that of airborne early warning, with the AWG-9 radar being used in an attempt to detect low-flying Iraqi strike aircraft.

Iran insists that its Tomcat fleet is still operational. Dismissing that he called 'unfounded reports by the media of global imperialism that only a few of the total 77 F-14 aircraft of the Islamic Republic were combat ready,' IRIAF Commander, Pilot Colonel Hushang Seddiq claimed on 12 December 1983 that the Iraqi Air Force was under no such illusion, and tried to avoid air combat. Reports of Tomcat unserviceability were 'false propaganda intended to boost the morale of Iraqi military personnel and of their lackeys,' said Iran.

Evidence that Tomcats might be available in more than nominal numbers came on 13 October 1984, when Chief of the Joint Staff Brig Gen Zahirnezhad, accompanied by Air Force Commander Seddiq visited the 'Eighth Fighter Base' in Esfahan for an inspection and to attend the

F-14s, while one widely-respected industry source—the Connecticut-based Defense Marketing Services—says that the weapon has been used in combat, downing Iraqi MiG-23s.

To some degree the US arms embargo has failed. Some US arms dealers have attempted to break their own government's embargo, but to date no aircraft or aircraft spares are known to have reached Iran via such sources—although a scheme foiled in August 1983 planned to sell more than $2 billion worth of weaponry including attack helicopters, rocket launchers, missiles and tanks. In August 1984 a US Federal Grand Jury charged an exporter with illegally shipping tank, APC and howitzer spares to Iran, plus spares for TOW anti-tank missiles.

With most Western nations following the US lead and avoiding arms sales to Iran, the Khomeini regime had no alternative but to turn to the international arms market, and to do business with almost anyone who might be able to supply badly-needed items of equipment. In 1980 only $400 million worth of arms were purchased, but this figure doubled in 1981 and reached $1.3 billion in 1983. Several third-party countries are known to have supplied US-manufactured arms and spares. North Korea, China and Brazil all proved major suppliers, but one of the most invaluable (if unlikely) sources of weaponry proved to be Israel.

In May 1982 the US State Department disclosed that Israel had supplied Iran with military equipment worth approximately $27 million. No further details of the hardware involved were given or dates for the transaction, but the latter is known to have included 250 replacement tyres for the IRIAF F-4 Phantom fleet. These were not new US-made tyres, but retread tyres supplied by Israel under a $300,000 contract.

Iran and Israel are officially hostile to one another, and have no diplomatic relations. Some sources suggest that many purchases from Israel may have been made through European arms dealers. At least one shipment of TOW anti-tank missiles is reported to have been made by Israel in November 1982 via European brokers.

In October 1984, the Iranian opposition organization Mojahedin-e Khalq, claimed to have obtained documents outlining Iranian–Israeli military co-operation. Arms, spare parts, ammunition and military hardware—including spare parts for Bell helicopters, F-4 Phantom, F-5E Tiger II and F-14 Tomcat fighters were being shipped, also Hawk, Sparrow, and Sidewinder missiles. This equipment was being air-freighted by three Israeli airlines—El Al, Kal cargo airlines, and Sandor. Once delivered to Frankfurt airport, the cargo is transferred to Iranian aircraft and flown to Tehran.

graduation ceremonies of newly-trained F-14 pilots. According to Teheran radio, Brig Gen Zahirnezhad '... gave out prizes and certificates to the graduating F-14 pilots, and letters of commendation to trainees and the industrious and committed personnel of the base who had played an active role in making F-14 planes operational.'

It is clear that Iranian pronouncements are not just propaganda. In the summer of 1984 Pentagon sources revised their estimates of Iranian Tomcat strength, saying that Iran may be operating 14–20 aircraft, maintaining them largely by cannibalization. The serviceability of Iran's AIM-54 Phoenix missiles remains another mystery. Tales of how the last Grumman personnel to leave Iran after the Revolution purloined—some versions say smashed or sabotaged—items of avionics needed in order to operate the Phoenix emerged soon after the event, and are still recounted at the company's Long Island facilities. US military intelligence now believes that some of the Phoenix missiles are being used on flyable

Two Tomcats refuel from one of the IIAF's Boeing 707 tankers. Note that the aircraft are unarmed. Recent reports indicate that the Iranians have restored some of their air-to-air refuelling capability
(Grumman)

Citing disaffected sources within Iran, the group claimed that arms flights took place every week on Monday, Wednesday, Friday and Saturday. The illicit cargoes were handled at gates 43, 30B and 45 at Frankfurt airport, 'remote areas ... in order to camouflage the activity and to allay suspicion,' the group claimed. The cargo was reloaded quickly onto Iranian aircraft. Two Iranian aircraft were assigned to collect the arms—a civilian cargo plane plus a civilian airliner which acted as a back-up in the event of technical troubles with the cargo aircraft. One shipment delivered to Frankfurt in April of that year had been flown in by South African Airlines, it was alleged. The South African plane unloaded its cargo directly onto an Iranian plane,' it was claimed.

The degree of faith which can be placed in such tales is questionable. Israel is certainly believed to be supporting Iran—presumably on the time-honoured principle that 'the enemy of my enemy is my friend'—but the prospect of significant quantities of F-14 spares being ordered via Israel seems minimal. Even the dimmest US State Department arms control official could presumably be relied on to realize that Israel does not operate Tomcats and does not require spares for the aircraft! Grumman sometimes does receive 'strange enquiries' concerning the Tomcat, but promptly refers these to the US Government.

In September 1983 Iranian Air Force Commander Colonel Mohammad Hasan Mo'inpur, admitted that sources of aircraft spares were extremely limited. 'Sometimes we find something in the free market,' he said. Tomcat spares were difficult to acquire, he confirmed. South Korea is reported to have supplied spare parts for F-4 and F-5 fighters, plus an unspecified quantity of Raytheon Hawk anti-aircraft missiles. Other reports mention Pakistan as a source of US-built weaponry. Iraqi intelligence also claims that the United Arab Emirates has re-exported at least $1 billion worth of arms to Iran.

Some munitions are being supplied by Third World arms industries—unspecified quantities of cluster bombs for use on Iranian aircraft formed part of shipments made by Israel in the early 1980s, and were included in a deal worth around $527,000 made in mid-1984 by Chilean manufacturer Cardoen. These deals are only part of a larger series of shipments which are supplying the Iranian war effort. Syria and Libya have provided Soviet-built equipment such as surface-to-air and anti-tank missiles, bombardment rockets, anti-aircraft guns, armoured personnel carriers, and small arms. Just before the outbreak of the Iran/Iraq war, Syria is reported to have flown to Iran via Turkey Soviet-made weaponry including 150 SAM-7 launchers with 600 missiles, plus 100 *Sagger* anti-tank missile launchers and 300 missiles.

The list of nations which have scrambled to fuel the Iranian war machine makes interesting reading. Few of these arms deals can be documented or confirmed, but several nations feature repeatedly. Soviet-built T-54, T-55 and T-62 tanks have been supplied by Libya, T-62 tanks by North Korea, TAM medium tanks by Argentina, M-60 tank spares by Israel, tank engines from the UK, and armoured cars by Brazil. Logistics ships have been delivered by the UK, plus *Combattante II*-class missile boats from France. Jeeps and trucks have been obtained from India, military electronics from the Netherlands.

Artillery has been supplied by Libya, ASTROS multiple rocket launchers by Brazil, mortars by North Korea, anti-aircraft guns from Israel, North Korea and Poland, and small arms from Argentina and North Korea, Israel, North Korea, and Libya have provided ammunition, while grenades have come in large numbers from Brazil.

In a parallel effort to such 'black' imports, Iran has been attempting—apparently with some success—to manufacture its own aircraft spares. Such 'reverse engineering' of spares is not uncommon in a world of conflicting political allegiances. Several Western companies are busy upgrading and rebuilding Soviet

bloc aircraft and missiles. Egypt for example is considering fitting some of its MiG-21 interceptors with Emerson radars and Raytheon AIM-7 Sparrow missiles, has copied the SA-7 *Grail* man-portable SAM and added a new and more reliable IR homing head, and has asked Thomson-CSF to fit a modern semi-automatic guidance system to the AT-3 *Sagger* anti-tank missile. Reverse-engineering of some F-14 spares by Israel's highly competent aircraft and electronics industry might even explain the reference to the F-14 in the Mojahedin-e Khalq group's claims detailed earlier.

Under a scheme intended to develop an indigenous defence manufacturing industry, the Shah's Government had entered into a series of co-production agreements, mostly with US companies, for the assembly and/or manufacture of aircraft, helicopters, missiles and electronic and electro-optical equipment. Like the major arms deals, these were cancelled after the Revolution. The demands of the current war have forced Iran to re-embark on the development of its arms industry, a programme which probably involves a degree of assistance from China, North

Like USN aircraft, Iranian Tomcats use the probe and drogue method of in-flight refuelling.
(Grumman)

Korea, and even Israel. In the days of the Shah, Iran's embryo aircraft industry had strong links with Israel Aircraft Industries. Given the existence of a documented 'Israeli Connection' in other areas of defence, it is possible that IAI may still be giving technical assistance in the creation of a limited but indigenous aerospace manufacturing capability. Here once again, claims must be treated with caution, but should not be dismissed out of hand.

The first priority was to improve Iranian maintenance skills. An Iranian radio broadcast in 1984 accused 'archsatan America' of having behaved during the Shah's regime 'as if they had embargoed every kind of information to the Iranian army about the manufacture and even the repair' of US-supplied weaponry. 'Whenever any of the said arms was damaged, it had to be repaired in the country where it had been manufactured ... or foreign experts would be called in to repair the damaged arms, so that they could be used again—millions of collars were spent on bringing in foreign experts.'

Faced with the need to keep its combat aircraft flying, the IRIAF had invested 11,000 manhours in a project to develop and apply indigenous repair schemes, listeners were told. 'Experts of the Iranian air force succeeded in repairing the bullet-riddled wings of F-4 aircraft and preparing them for combat'.

The same programme also claimed that Iranian technicians were 'repairing the Phoenix missile launching systems of the F-14'.

In December 1982 Iranian Defence Minister Col Mohammad Salimi was able to announce that the Islamic Republic was able to carry out full maintenance and repair on the F-14, and that 80 per cent of the components required were obtainable from domestic sources. (The latter figure presumably refers to mechanical parts only—Iran is unlikely to be able to obtain many of the specialized electronic components used in the Tomcat's avionics). Longer-term goal was 100 per cent of all components, he stated. In an interview with the newspaper *Jomhuri-ye Eslami* (Islamic Republic), he stated that basic repairs of Boeing 707 aircraft would start in March 1983.

Further reports were soon to follow. 'In the area of aircraft industries we have achieved significant success by developing a capability for producing

This is believed to be the first picture published in the West of an F-14A Tomcat (3-6020) in the markings of the Islamic Republic of Iran Air Force (IRIAF). Recent reports indicate that of the 80 Tomcats delivered to Iran, 25 aircraft are still operational and capable of flying air combat missions against Iraq in the Gulf War

sophisticated parts of airplanes, installing certain aircraft ammunition and weapons such as aircraft guns and missiles upon helicopters,' the Iranian Defence Minister stated on 30 September 1983. The Tomcat was singled out for special mention, with a claim that a locally produced substitute brake mechanism was more efficient than the 'official' US-designed component. A few days later, an exhibition called 'From Karbala to Jerusalem' held at Tehran's grand prayer ground included Iranian-manufactured spare parts for the F-14, F-5, and F.27 and C-130 transports. Also featured was a display highlighting F-14 operations, and components from downed Iraqi Sukhoi fighters.

In September of the same year the managing director of the Defence Industries' Organization claimed that many spare parts for the F-14, F-4, and F-5 were being manufactured. Speaking at a Press conference in Tehran, he announced plans for the indigenous manufacture of helicopters and aircraft, naval craft, and military vehicles. Before the revolution only foreign technicians were allowed to work on IIAF aircraft, he stated, but the servicing of fighters and helicopters was now being handled by Iranian personnel. 'Before the Islamic revolution we were not permitted to repair many weapons. They were returned to their foreign manufacturers for repairs,' explained Colonel Sattari, commander of the Iranian Army's artillery training centre. 'But now a great deal of this repair work is carried out at this centre. Some work has been carried out on the repair and adjustment of our defence radar systems.'

To what degree the above is coloured by the need for wartime propaganda is unclear. The concept that any newly created aerospace industry could keep an aircraft as complex as the F-14 operational without the manufacturer's support, and expatriate technical expertize let alone manufacture spares seems difficult to credit. One Western aerospace engineer, recently returned from the Middle East as the above account was being prepared described the Iranian claims as 'rubbish'. He had no direct evidence to offer, just the hard-won experience of trying to maintain simple subsonic jets under similar conditions with full manufacturer's support!

The fact remains, however, that Iran does have a small but growing aircraft industry. On 17 October 1984 Iranian Prime Minister Mir Hoseyn Musavi inspected the aerospace operations of Iran's Defence Industries Organization, visiting hangars used for repairs to the F-14, F-4, F-5, P-3 and C-130, plus the associated engine-test bays. Iran plans to expand its aerospace industry, it was announced. Mir Hoseyn Musavi stressed that the aerospace workers were as important as front-line combatants, and thanked the staff for working around the clock despite the organization's financial problems and cramped facilities.

Some scanty evidence of Iranian Tomcat operations appears in the form of combat reports from the long-running war. Iran has never released details of any Tomcat 'kills', but Iraqi pilots have on several occasions reported downing F-14s. Such claims lack the exaggerated element which has so often in the past marked air combat claims from the Middle East. Iraqi claims are occasional and unspectacular, a fact which at first sight lends them some credence.

Whether Iranian aircraft were in fact downed on each occasion is impossible to tell, positive identification during the heat of combat can be difficult. In theory, the simple rule of 'if it's got two tails, it's a Tomcat' should work, but the practical hazards and pressures of combat make enemy aircraft identification more of an art than a science. Previous wars have shown two factors which always must be borne in mind when assessing 'kill' claims—pilots tend to over-claim, and have a habit of reporting that the aircraft shot down was the latest and best type that the enemy currently fields.

In March 1982, a downed Iranian pilot is reported to have told his captors, 'We were really surprised to see an Iraqi MiG-21 shoot down the very sophisticated F-14,' commenting that this indicated a high level of Iraqi pilot training. Iran was surprised to see Iraqi aircraft flying deep into its territory and overflying Tehran.

Tomcat seems to have played a significant role during the 1983 naval actions in the beleaguered Gulf waterway, as Iraq attempted to stop the flow of oil tankers to and from Iran's oil terminal at Kharg Island. On 11 September 1983, Iraqi aircraft were reported in action against enemy positions 'in both the battle zone and deep inside Iran in the northern sector'. Two Iranian Tomcats attempting to intercept the attackers were shot down in flames near Marivan.

On the morning of 4 October Iraqi aircraft attacked 'an enemy maritime target' in the northeast of the Arabian Gulf, setting the vessel on fire. Returning to the area several hours later, Iraqi fighters entered a dogfight against two Iranian Tomcats at 15.45. One was shot down, crashing into the sea, while the other broke off the engagement, fleeing back to base.

At dawn on 21 November 1983 Iraqi naval units had sighted 'enemy maritime targets' moving from Kharg Island towards Khowr-e Musa in order to enter Bandar-e Khomeyni. An attack was carried out with air support, leading to the claimed downing of an F-14 in a dogfight over the Bahragan area, and the destruction of seven vessels. According to Iraqi news reports, all Iraqi aircraft and naval craft had returned safely to base. Speaking on Iraqi radio, the commander of the Iraqi Navy claimed that the day's action had refuted the Iranian regime's lies and deceptions regarding the alleged safe passage between Kharg Island and Bandar-e Khomeyni.

No further Tomcat kills were claimed until the following spring, when during an air battle in Iranian airspace on the morning of 24 February, an F-14 was reported shot down at 9.45 am in a dogfight over

Khafajiyah (Susangerd)—the action described at the beginning of this chapter.

At dawn on 1 July, an Iranian convoy was discovered in the Khowr-e Musa zone in the north-eastern part of the Arabian Gulf trying to enter Bandar-e Khomeyni. It was intercepted by the Iraqi Navy, which accounced the destruction of 'five maritime targets' during a series of attacks. Two Iranian vessels apparently fled the area, only to be destroyed in an Iraqi minefield. In an attempt to provide air cover for the beleaguered convoy, Iran sent in jet fighters, and in the resulting air combat, the Iraqi Air Force claimed an F-14 'seen crashing into the sea' at 10.15 am local time. The remaining Iranian aircraft broke off combat and fled, said Iraq. Iran later confirmed that its ships had been attacked, but denied losing an F-14. According to a spokesman for the War Information headquarters of the Supreme Defence Council, all the Iranian aircraft had returned to their bases safely after carrying out their missions. Iraq's claim was 'a mere lie', listeners were told.

If Iraqi claims are correct, 11 August proved an even greater disaster for Iran's Tomcat fleet. At dawn on that day, an Iranian convoy escorted by fighter aircraft was detected in the Khowr-e Musa area in the north-eastern part of the Arabian Gulf. The Iranian formation was apparently heading for the port of Bandar Khomeini at the northern extremity of the Gulf, but during a co-ordinated attack by Iraqi aircraft and warships, five Iranian vessels were left burning and sinking, while the associated air battle saw three F-14s shot down.

A repeated Iraqi warning issued the next day told ships sailing to Iranian ports to expect attack. This renewed declaration, and the news that a Greek-owned supertanker had been damaged in an earlier attack on 7 August, led to a hastily-announced meeting of the Saudi Arabian-led Gulf Co-operation Council to meet to discuss ways of ending the war.

On the 11 February 1985, graphic evidence of IRIAF strength was given by a mass flypast over Tehran's Azadi Square. Air Force Commander Colonel Hushang Seddiq later announced in a radio broadcast that a total of 79 aircraft had taken part, including 13 F-5 Tiger IIs, 12 F-4 Phantoms and no less than 25 F-14 Tomcats. At the time of the display, many other Iranian fighters were deployed in the war zones and on air alert to guard the capital, he added. The flypast '... proved the weakness of Western intelligence and espionage sources because of their baseless assumptions of Iran's military might,' said Seddiq. 'Some four years have passed since the war began and during this time we have not relied on either of the super-powers.'

As this text was finalized, the war continued, with yet another Iranian offensive having failed. Despite the reports of Tomcat availability, the Grumman warplane was not reported in action. Either the aircraft was not being flown, or else the Tomcat pilots suffered no losses.

Faced with the smuggling of spares and other military hardware to Iran, the US Government decided to crack down on the offenders, launching a programme which included wiretapping, long-running undercover operations, and the creation of at least one 'front' business intended to attract the attention of potential smugglers. The latter included Ameritech, set up in Irvine, California, by the US Customs. In the 12 months during which this book was researched and written, the US authorities have detected eight attempts to smuggle equipment to Iran. Some were relatively small-scale operations, but a major goal of the investigation was to uncover the supply routes used for sophisticated weapon systems such as missiles for Iran's fighters and surface-to-air missile batteries, and high-technology spares for the Tomcat and Phantom fleets.

On 9 January 1985, the Ameritech 'sting' paid off—Portuguese businessmen Moises Broder, Eduardo Ojeda, and Carlos Ribeiro, were arrested at Los Angeles International Airport, when Federal agents seized a $619,300 shipment of Hawk missile parts and classified components for radar equipments. These had apparently been purchased from Ameritech. All three men pleaded guilty when tried on 13 May.

Like the US, Britain had been a major supplier of arms to the Shah, and it soon became obvious that the UK was involved—without the consent of its Government—as a centre for the illicit supply of weaponry to the Revolutionary regime. At least five smuggling routes have involved London, either as a shipping location or financial centre, claimed a report in the British newspaper the Sunday Times. Iran's UK-based contacts with would-be suppliers have been maintained via the National Iranian Oil Company, whose building also houses IRIAF and Iranian Navy personnel.

Around the time of the Ameritech arrests, the US Customs Service asked the assistance of the FBI in dealing with an arms smuggling route which ran via London. By using court-ordered wiretaps, Federal authorities had infiltrated an alleged ring of arms smugglers, and discovered that sophisticated equipment had been stolen for illegal export to Iran. FBI Director William H Webster was later to explain that 'the aircraft parts were being shipped under the guise of automobile parts or medical supplies.'

On Thursday 11 July Britain and the US started the job of winding up this illicit flow of arms. On that day, the Customs authorities in the UK arrested the first suspect—an Iranian national. The next day, the FBI pounced on the US end of the alleged smuggling route. Three men were arrested by FBI agents in San Diego, California, one more in New York.

Primitivo Baluyat Cayabyab, a US Navy enlisted man assigned to duties as an aviation storekeeper, was taken into custody from the aircraft carrier Kitty Hawk, then based at San Diego. Also arrested was Pedro Manansala Quito, a civilian warehouse worker at the Navy's North Island Supply Department,

Fleet Avionics Logistics Support Center, San Diego.

The man arrested in New York was Edgardo Pangilinan Agustin, a Filipino businessman who is retired from the US Navy. The FBI claimed that Agustin and the Iranian national being held by the British were doing business in San Diego. The fifth arrest was that of Agustin's · brother—Franklin Pangilinan Agustin—in San Diego. The FBI were not able to release the name of the Iranian arrested in London, since British law forbids the release of the name of arrested suspects until charges have formally been made.

All five were charged with violating a US Statute prohibiting the interstate transportation of stolen property, the theft of US Government property, and violation of the US Arms Exports and Imports Act. A spokesman for the United States customs said he believed the only motivation for the thefts was money. FBI Director Webster said the investigation was continuing and 'will include interviews of active duty and retired US Navy personnel.'

Kitty Hawk, due to sail on Wednesday 24 July became the centre of controversy when a US Navy auditor, Petty Officer 1st Class Robert Jackson, took the dramatic step of sending a telegram to President Reagan in an attempt to have the deployment delayed. Jackson explained in his telegram that he believed that he had discovered how spare aircraft parts were diverted from the carrier and the Navy supply system.

'I have discovered the means by which Iran and (the) USSR were able to steal F-14 parts and Phoenix missile system components from the USS *Kitty Hawk*', Jackson told the President. 'I believe a thorough investigation of this matter is crucial to national security. Please halt the USS Kitty Hawk.' If the ship were allowed to sail, '. . . valuable evidence necessary to the investigation of my charges will be altered and destroyed'.

In a statement sent to the FBI, US Navy investigators and Democratic Congressman Jim Bates of California, Jackson also alleged that spare parts worth millions of dollars were unaccounted for, accusing *Kitty Hawk* crew members of stealing Navy equipment and parts, dumping excess military supplies into the ocean, and falsifying records to conceal these abuses.

US Defense Secretary Caspar W Weinberger told Bates on 23 July that the carrier would have to sail on the 24th as planned (it was apparently due to relieve *Constellation*, which was then on deployment in the Indian Ocean). Investigations were continuing, Bates was assured, and the Pentagon's Inspector General was to particpate. The FBI had by that time arrested seven suspects, including three USN employees, while agents had traced stolen spares back to two other carriers—*Carl Vinson* and *Ranger*.

Little more than a week after *Kitty Hawk* put to sea, time apparently ran out on a third smuggling route which was intended to supply the IRIAF with other vitally-needed equipment including Phoenix missiles and F-4 Phantom spares. As the result of a long undercover operation by the US authorities, the FBI was able to arrest six people—including a US Army officer—on 1 August. The arrests took place in Florida, California and Virginia, before any equipment had been shipped.

The accused were Lt Col Wayne G Gillespie (at that time assigned to the US Army's Missile Command at the Pentagon), Paul Sjeklocha—also known as Paul Cutter—a California-based publisher and author of articles on military science and technology, Fadel M Fadel, a Lebanese national engaged in import-export business in Calabasas, California, his wife Farhin Sanai, George Neranchi of California, and Amir Hosseni, who claimed to be an official of the Iranian Government. (The FBI has since suggested that he is an Iranian procurement officer). The FBI was also looking for weapons dealer Charles St Clair of Granda Hills, California. He was out of the country at the time of the arrest of the other five, but flew back to the USA from London on 5 August, and was duly arrested. All were charged with conspiracy to violate the arms export control act rather than with individual violations of the act.

According to FBI Director William H Webster and Customs Commissioner William von Raab, the accused intended to buy a variety of US missiles including AIM-54 Phoenix, AIM-9 Sidewinder, the AIM-7F and -7M versions of Sparrow, TOW anti-tank weapons, and the Harpoon anti-ship missile. They were alleged to have tried to obtain French-built Exocet anti-ship missiles, plus spares for the F-4 Phantom—including 10 General Electric J79 engines. This was no small scale operation—the planned TOW purchase was for 1,140 rounds at a total cost of $9.12 million, and the accused had apparently agreed to provide an aircraft to fly the weapons and parts to Iran.

In most of the cases listed above, it is difficult to tell how much equipment reached Iran. 'As far as we know, nothing really reached Iran,' a Justice Department source told the *Los Angeles Times* several days after the arrest of Cayabyab from *Kitty Hawk* and his associates. The alleged ring had been infiltrated early enough for authorities to plant phony equipment among the shipments, said the newspaper. An account from the *Washington Post* was less optimistic, reporting that '. . . the smuggling ring has spanned several years, and has been able to export untold amounts of parts before being detected'. Shipments intercepted by the investigators over a seven-month period beginning in late 1984 included 'over a dozen cartons . . . and over two dozen separate parts', including some valued at more than $50,000.

Most of the cases above had not come to trial as this text was finally completed, so it is too early to say whether or not the 'Iranian Connection' has finally been broken—at least as far as the F-14 is concerned. The full truth will perhaps never be known.

Chapter 6
Breeding a better Tomcat

With the F-14 in widespread US Navy service, and in at least limited Iranian service, the Grumman fighter's story seemed likely to be a dull one, with none of the variants or spectacular sales associated with the F-4 Phantom. By the late 1970s, several nations had evaluated the Tomcat, but none of these evaluations resulted in a sale. Israel, Saudia Arabia and Japan considered the aircraft as an alternative to the F-15, but all opted for the single-seat McDonnell Douglas fighter.

Although offered to the Australian, Canadian and Spanish air forces—three nations in the market for new fighters around the end of the decade—all opted for the McDonnell Douglas F/A-18A. Cost seems to have been the main factor which told against the Tomcat, although Israel is reported to have considered the type too large and complex for its style of operations. One Israeli pilot is reported to have counted the moving parts in the Tomcat's wing and glove system, then decided that he'd prefer to go to war in something simpler.

Even the British Royal Air Force was at one time seen as a potential customer. Faced with rising costs of the planned Tornado Air Defence Variant (now in production as the Tornado F.2) the British MoD looked at the F-14, F-15 and F-16. It concluded that only the F-14 would meet Britain's defence needs; the F-15 lacked the two-seat cockpit and facilities required for interception in the face of massive ECM, and the F-16 was simply too small. Given the prospective price tag of Tomcat, Tornado seemed the best bet.

The slow timescale of the ADV project was another problem. 'The Few have never been fewer' was how one newspaper summed up the fact that in the late 1970s the UK was defended by less than 100 fighters. The British Press actually seemed surprised by the miniscule size of the UK's run-down defences—perhaps they thought that the long series of defence 'reviews' (polite euphemism for 'cuts') which British Governments of all political persuasions had inflicted on the British armed forces were theoretical exercises.

Once again, the prospect of an RAF Tomcat buy was discussed. One method of lowering the bill might be to buy second-hand examples from the US Navy, or even from Iran. Enquiries were in fact made, but the MoD was keen to dismiss these as unauthorized and the work of low-level officers once the story made the pages of the daily newspapers. At an air show several weeks later, Grumman asked the defence editor of the British weekly magazine *Flight International* if in his opinion the RAF was really interested in Tomcat. The company was faced with the decision on whether it should invest significant time and effort in chasing a possible sale. 'It's funny you should ask me that—I was about to ask you the same question!' he replied. 'The fact that you are asking *me* answers *it*, I think.'

For a while the run-down state of the RAF was still considered headline news, but eventually it sank into obscurity. Tornado ADV would be in service by 1982, perhaps 1983, so the 'fighter gap' would only last for a few more years. *No slippage in ADV timescale would be tolerated*, the author was assured in 1979 by a Conservative politician. If Panavia could not deliver the goods on time, the Government would consider buying US fighters. He may have believed that the threat to 'buy US' could be used to keep the ADV programme up to speed, but I did not. Maintaining timescales is not something that Europe's ailing aircraft manufacturers are very good at. At the time of writing (June 1985) Tornado ADV is still not in squadron service. The only US fighters ordered in the interim were a batch of ex-USN F-4J Phantoms taken into service to make up for the stationing of Spey-engined Phantoms in the Falklands after the 1982 conflict with Argentina.

All the wealthier air arms having now chosen their new fighters, the prospect of another F-14 customer seems remote. Tomcat's capabilities are beyond the pocket of most nations, and no attempts are currently being made to sell Tomcat to overseas air arms.

Silliest story in the Tomcat sales saga must be the alleged Greek order. Much to the surprise of the world's aviation Press (and one suspects, to the surprise of Grumman), the British newspaper the *Sunday Times* claimed in July 1984 that the US Government had decided to suspend the shipment of a consignment of 15 second-hand F-14 aircraft to Greece. The article alleged that Washington had frozen delivery of the Tomcats as part of a series of measures intended to show US displeasure at the Papandreou Government's opposition to the deployment of US nuclear missiles in Europe.

Greece was at the time shopping for new fighters to match Turkey's planned acquisition of the F-16 Fighting Falcon, and had repeatedly postponed selection of a new aircraft, but Tomcat was never a serious contender—the shortlist of types under consideration was soon reduced to the Mirage 2000, F-16, F-18A Hornet and Panavia Tornado. At no time had the Grumman warplane been a contender, and within days of the article appearing, Greek Government spokesman Dhimitrios Maroudhas stated that the story bore 'no relation whatsoever to reality. Our country has never ordered F-14 aircraft from the United States. It must also be emphasized that what the *Sunday Times* reports on the so-called freezing of the sale of military aircraft to Greece by the United States is also untrue. No order from the United States is pending.' Later that year, the Greek Government eliminated Tornado from the competition, and after yet another postponment of its decision, finally opted for a mix of Mirage 2000 and F-16 fighters.

Perhaps the biggest missed opportunity was in the mid-1970s, when the US Air Force was in the market for a new interceptor to replace the 20-year-old F-106 Delta Darts used by Aerospace Defense Command. Follow-On Interceptor (FOI) was intended for deployment in the continental USA. The USAF always favoured the F-15 Eagle for the FOI role, since this fighter was already in its inventory, but a modest F-14 buy would have made good sense. The F-15 was not able to match the Tomcat's multiple target tracking and multiple missile-launch capabilities, or the long-range firepower of the Phoenix. For the FOI mission, Phoenix would be two to three times as effective as the AIM-7F version of Sparrow, Grumman claimed.

The USAF was ordered to consider alternatives such as the F-14, F-16 and F/A-18, but not surprisingly decided to stay with the F-15. The F-14 could have been built from scratch at a unit cost of around $24 million, or obtained at lower cost by repurchasing the Iranian fleet. Studies showed that rebuilt Iranian aircraft would cost around $13 million

to $14 million each. In 1977, General Daniel James, commander-in-chief of North American Air Defense Command proposed the purchase of F-14s. Two years later, his successor, General James E Hill formally asked the Pentagon to consider the F-14, stating that earlier USAF studies had shown the Tomcat to be the most effective aircraft for the interceptor mission in terms of performance. A force of around 170 would have been needed to re-equip ADC's interceptor wings.

One change which the aircraft would need for the overland mission was the addition of a medium PRF to augment the existing high and low rates. Without this, the aircraft could have blind spots in its radar coverage when overtaking targets flying over land. Other changes would have minimal. A USAF-style flight-refuelling receptacle could have been added on the glove section of the wing, while HF radio would be added to the communications fit.

Much of the USAF's existing support equipment was compatible with the F-14, said Grumman. By means of adaptors, the Bendix automatic test equipment used to test F-15 avionics could handle around 137 of the Tomcat's 189 line-replaceable units, while mechanical support equipment already in USAF service would cope with many routine Tomcat maintenance tasks, except those involving the Phoenix and its launcher, the escape system, and structural repair. The TF30 was already in the USAF inventory, while maintenance of specialized systems such as the Phoenix could perhaps have been handled with assistance from the Navy to avoid costly duplication of support facilities.

Studies showed that at 1975 prices, a 170-strong F-14 force would cost $4,300 million, compared with $3,900 million for the same number of F-15s. In practice, a force of around 290 Eagles would have been needed to provide the capability of 170 F-14s. A Grumman study suggested that given a massive *Backfire* raid on the USA in which it was assumed that the attackers would use ECM but would not release decoys, the F-14A would score 50 per cent more bomber kills than the same number of F-15As, and would also be able to destroy many Soviet air-to-surface missiles.

Another study considered four interceptors attacking a bomber prepared to take maximum evasive action. It was assumed that once the bomber detected the fighter's AI radar transmissions, it would release four decoys, then begin jinking. The results of 100 simulated engagements suggested that the F-14 would have a 70 per cent kill rate, while the F-15 would manage less than 40 per cent. One factor ignored in this scenario was the use of the E-3A AWACS to support the fighters.

Should the USAF wish such a facility, Grumman could provide a datalink which would allow flights of F-14s to exchange track file information from each other's radar systems. This would cope with instances when Tomcat detected targets at the extremities of the 200 nm detection scan width of the AWG-9. Some aircraft could take on one group of targets, while information on the remainder could be passed to another Tomcat formation.

The disadvantages of operating a specialized interceptor, plus what was probably more than a degree of resistance to purchasing yet another US Navy type, counted against the Tomcat. Some studies were made of two-seat Phoenix-armed F-15 FOI designs, but addition of the Navy missile would have added an aerodynamic penalty and been expensive. Estimated development cost of a Phoenix-equipped F-15 was around $500 million. The aircraft eventually deployed to defend US airspace were standard F-15As.

The US Navy had always planned to 'improve the breed', but for a long time these plans seemed doomed to failure. Follow-on to the cancelled F-14B should have been the F-14C, an F401-powered aircraft equipped with more advanced electronic equipment and weapons systems. This project, too, was shelved.

Plans for re-engining Tomcat were re-investigated in the mid-1970s, but shortages of funds effectively resulted in this project being stillborn. One useful end result of this work was that the Navy decided to co-operate with the USAF in developing a new fighter engine. Both services were becoming con-

cerned that Pratt & Whitney had come to dominate the market for high-thrust fighter engines. The F100 on which the USAF's F-15 and F-16 programmes depended was still not clear of technical problems, but GE had no alternative fighter engine to offer—the company's most powerful fighter engine was the F404 which developed only 16,000 lb (7258 kg) of afterburning thrust. The two services decided to pool their limited funds and order GE to develop a new high-thrust fighter engine. This would maintain the company's expertise in fighter-engine technology, provide a back-up to the troubled F100, and perhaps even an alternative engine for Tomcat.

The obvious starting point for a modest development programme was the F101 engine flying in the B-1 bomber. Developed from 1965 onwards under the USAF's Advanced Turbine Engine Gas Generator programme, the F101 used advanced technology to reduce exhaust emissions, lessen noise and reduce fuel consumption. High turbine temperatures were used in order to give good engine performance and efficiency, but high levels of durability and reliability were also demanded.

Following tests with rival GE and P&W demonstrator engines developed under this $72 million R&D programme, GE was selected in June 1970 to develop 40 prototype engines for the B-1. Testing of core engines began in October 1971, and the first complete F101 was ready for trials in April 1972. Preliminary qualification testing was completed in October 1973, and the first test engine was delivered in January of the following year. First flight of a B-1 prototype was on 23 December 1974, and on 10 April 1975 supersonic flying was under way. The engine passed its critical design review in August 1975, and initial purchase of long-lead production items was begun. Product verification testing was completed in the autumn of 1976 and GE seemed all set to manufacture more than 1,100 engines, but in June 1977 President Carter terminated the B-1 programme after only four aircraft had been built. Resurrection of the B-1 under President Reagan resulted in a new F101 version. Generally similar to the -100 used on the B-1A prototypes, the F101-200 incorporates modifications intended to match the engine to the B-1B mission, and to increase durability.

In March 1979, GE was awarded a $79.7 million, 30-month contract to develop and build three F101 DFE (Derivative Fighter Engine) powerplants. The new engine was to be a 27,000 lb (12,250 kg) thrust turbofan based on the F101 engine of the B-1 bomber and incorporating components such as a scaled-up fan, and modified afterburner and nozzle from the smaller F404 used by the F/A-18A Hornet. Like the

Samurai cat: this artist's sketch for a Tomcat decal was created at a time when Japan was seen as a potential market for the F-14

OPPOSITE PAGE
Tomcat wears Canadian 'maple leaf' markings during its evaluation by the Canadian Armed Forces (Grumman)

F101-200, this was able to take advantage of continued engineering development of the basic F101 carried out between 1976 and 1981 with the intention of maturing the design and extending engine life.

The F101 DFE drew upon experience already gained in 1977 and 1978 with two F101-X demonstrator engines which had clocked up 350 hours of ground running. Three F101 DFE engines were built, their serial numbers 003, 004 and 005 emphasizing commonality with the F101-X demonstrators. The first was used for systems testing, the second for accelerated mission testing, while the third was shipped to the Navy's Air Propulsion Test Center at Trenton, New Jersey for simulated high-altitude testing. Trials went well. After 1000 hours of running under fighter-type conditions, 004 was stripped down, inspected, re-assembled, then put through a further 1,000 hours of running, this time in test cycles designed to simulate F-14 operations.

This gruelling check-out was finally completed in the summer of 1981, clearing the engines for flight testing in the F-14 and F-15. Flight tests in an F-16 testbed started in December 1981 and were com-

pleted in five months. Twenty pilots flew the aircraft, building up a total of 75 flight hours in 58 sorties. Engine trimming was not required, and the pilots were able to fly the Fighting Falcon without regard for engine performance or throttle position. Simulated air-to-air, air-to-ground and interdiction missions were flown, while a series of ground based test runs measured the infrared signature of the modified aircraft. Performance testing included sustained turns, climbs in military and maximum power, and wind-up turns.

'Early in the programme, a few slow augmentor light-offs in a small thumbprint region on the left-hand side of the flight envelope were quickly resolved by increasing the pilot fuel burner fuel-air ratio in this region,' said F101 project manager George Ward. 'After this adjustment, successful lights were achieved with minimum flight speeds at altitudes from 5,000 to 50,000 ft (1500–15,000 m).'

While the F-16 trials were under way, the original No 7 prototype Tomcat was brought out of storage, fitted with the new powerplants, and given the unofficial designation 'Super Tomcat'. A three-month flight-test programme started on 14 July 1982. Given the thrust which its designers had originally hoped for, Tomcat could really show it paces, encouraging the Navy to order a further 70 hours of test flying. This was completed in March 1982, causing the service to give serious consideration to re-

This desk model, and a set of files in the Grumman archives, are all that remain of the proposed USAF air defence Tomcat
(Grumman)

engining the Tomcat.

In October 1982 formal development of the F101 DFE was begun, but the engine by now had a rival for the F-14's favours—Pratt & Whitney's PW1128 high-thrust derivative of the F-100. By 1982, events were moving fast. In the summer of that year the Air Force decided to adopt an alternative engine for the F-15 and F-16, splitting future purchases of around 1000 engines needed between Fiscal Years 1985 to 1987 between Pratt & Whitney and GE. Competition between the two engine companies would provide the commercial pressure needed to make GE and P&W trim their prices for servicing and spares, while maintaining two engine production lines.

With new Soviet fighters such as the MiG-29 *Fulcrum* and Su-27 *Flanker* about to enter service, the US Navy knew that the need for improved aircraft was becoming more urgent. With President Reagan's determination to build the US Navy up to a strength of 15 carriers, the most obvious way of providing the necessary air power was by adapting existing designs such as the F-14 and A-6 Intruder. The USN announced that it too would move to competitive engine evaluations in selecting a new powerplant for Tomcat.

Initially the candidates for the Navy programme were the GE F110 and the P&W PW1128. Although both companies were offered late-model F-14s for mock-up fit checks, the US Navy decided in the summer of 1983 to abandon this plan, and to rely on

Tomcat would have been an ideal replacement for the aging F-106 Delta Darts of Aerospace Defense Command (ADC), but inter-service rivalry ruled out a USAF Tomcat buy
(S Black)

the results of the USAF's competitive evaluation.

On 18 May 1983, the engine competition was formally begun when the USAF issued a request for proposals to both companies. The two candidate engines offered to the USAF were the GE F101 DFE (now re-designated F110), and a revised P&W F100 with a digital electronic engine control, longer life core and other improvements. In February 1983, the USAF Aeronautical Systems Division at Wright-Patterson AFB awarded GE a $109.3 million contract for full-scale development of the F110. In designing the F110, GE designers had aimed to create an engine without throttle restrictions, and tough enough to operate for eight years without overhaul under average USAF operational requirements. During Air Force qualification tests, a production F110 was subjected to 4,400 TAC cycles, the equivalent of more than 2,000 flight hours.

When the first competitive engine buy was announced by the USAF on 3 February 1984, the result was a surprise for the pundits. Instead of being awarded the smaller portion of the FY85 engine orders, GE carried off a massive 75 per cent of the total, 120 F110 engines for all but 30 of the FY85 production run of F-16 fighters. FY85 F-15 Eagles and the remaining FY85 F-16s would use the F100 in its new and upgraded form. Although both power-plants had met the technical requirements, the F110 had greater thrust and promised to have lower overall support costs, said the USAF. The F110 was to be phased into the General Dynamics aircraft production line as soon as production engines become available, but individual USAF units would never operate a 'mix' of engine types, choice of engine would be made at wing level. (F110s ordered a year later in the 54:46 per cent split of FY86 are also for service in the F-16, but future models of the F-15 would be designed to accept the F110 or the F100.) High altitude testing was completed at the Arnold

Engineering and Development Center in Tullahoma, Tennessee by the end of 1984, clearing the engine for production deliveries, initially to GD for use in the F-16C.

F-16 export clients were quick to change to the F110. Israeli defence minister Moshe Arens announcement in the summer of 1084 that the Fighting

F-14B

Falcons due to be purchased by the IDFAF in 1986 would be F110-powered. A Turkish announcement favouring the F110 was quick to follow, so this engine will be fitted to the 160 F-16s due for delivery to Turkey starting in 1987.

By this time the USN has announced its own decision. On 7 February the service delivered another blow to P&W by adopting the F110 for Tomcats due for delivery from 1988 onwards. Having adopted the F110, the USN will stick with the GE engine, and has no plans for USAF-style annual procurement competitions. The bill for developing and flight testing a navalized version of the F110 is likely to be $150 million spread over five years.

In August 1984 the Navy awarded Grumman a $1140 million contract for development of improved versions of the F-14 and A-6. Over a 57 month period, the company was to develop, integrate and evaluate a series of improvements to the Tomcat's radar, avionics and powerplant, creating the F-14D. The troublesome TF30 was to be replaced with the F110, the avionics were to be upgraded from analogue to digital to permit integration of current and future systems, the aircraft receiving an enhanced radar, new computer, stores management system, controls, displays, and digital INS.

The F110 is a compact engine 181 inch (460 cm) in length, and 46.5 inch (118 cm) in diameter. It weighs 3,830 lb (1737 kg). The annular intake incorporates a bullet-dome spinner and 20 fixed radial vanes with variable trailing flaps. Hot bleed air is used for anti-icing. The original F101 had a two-stage axial fan with a pressure ratio of 2.3 to 1 and a mass airflow of around 250 lb/sec (160 kg/sec). For the F110, a three-stage fan with a pressure ratio of more than 3 to 1 handles a mass flow of around 270 lb/sec (122 kg/sec). Variable inlet guide vanes are located forward from the fan, which has solid titanium blades. Bypass ratio is approximately 0.87 to 1.

The first three stages of the axial-flow compressor are made from titanium, the remaining six from 8286 steel. Sprayed-on shround materials are used—aluminium, bronze and nickel-graphite on the first six stages, and Metco 442 nickel-graphite on the final three. Overall pressure ratio is up to 11 to 1.

The annular combustion chamber is short, and designed for smokeless operation. Made from machined Hastelloy X, it has 20 dual-cone fuel injectors and swirl-cup vaporizers. Hot efflux passes to a single-stage HP turbine with convective and film-cooled blades and vanes manufactured from Rene 125. Turbine inlet temperature is approximately 2,500 degrees F (1,370 C). Blades are individually replaceable, without rotor disassembly.

The F401-powered F-14B was to have been the definitive Tomcat. The sole prototype is seen here on final approach to Calverton Field
(Grumman)

Re-engined with General Electric F101 DFE engines, the sole F-14B prototype was used to test this bomber-derived powerplant (Grumman)

From the HP turbine, the efflux passes to an uncooled LP turbine of two-stage configuration, then to a fully-modulated afterburner in which hot gas from the core section is mixed with fan air. When afterburning is selected, fuel is injected into both the fan and core ducts and mixed prior to combustion. Scaled up from the design used on the F404 engine of the F/A-18A Hornet, the variable-area exhaust duct of the F110 is made from welded titanium.

The version of the engine to be used in the Tomcat is the F110-GE-400. This has an 82 per cent commonality by parts with the USAF's F110-GE-100, and 50 per cent commonality by cost. Engine reliability of the naval F110 promises to be excellent. Hot-end inspection life will be 1,500 hours, almost double the 880 hours of the TF30-P-414A and nearly three times that of the -414.

The biggest difference between the F110 and the TF30 are the mechanical adaptations needed to match the new engine with the Tomcat airframe. The TF30 is 233.5 inch (593 cm) long, but the basic F110-GE-100 measures only 181 inch (460 cm) from front face to nozzle outlet. If the front face were to be mated with the exiting inlet, the nozzle would be wrongly positioned, while moving the engine aft to get the nozzle in the correct location would require modifications to the proven and trouble-free inlet system, and disturb the aircraft's centre of gravity.

For the Tomcat F101 DFE flight tests, Grumman wanted to get the new engine into the air at a minimum of cost and time, so simply followed the second approach, adding ballast in the nose of the aircraft to keep the centre of gravity within acceptable limits. This crude scheme was obviously not acceptable for a production fighter, but an ingenious solution devised by GE and the Navy involves 'stretching' the engine by 50 inches (127 cm). This has been done by adding a new section between the engine and the afterburner section. This creates no significant engineering difficulties; the problem in afterburner design is when the customer demands that the unit be made shorter!

By means of this simple parallel-sided adaptor, which incorporates a central section for the core exhaust, surrounded by an annular duct for the fan airflow, the front face of the F110 is moved forward by 39 inches (99 cm) to mate with the existing inlet ducting, while the nozzle is positioned 11 inches (28 cm) further aft. The revised nozzle location should reduce the aerodynamic drag of the boat-tail area of the rear fuselage.

Forward mounting point of the TF30 is some 30 inches (76 cm) behind the intake, while that of the F110 is higher up the side of the engine and only 10 inches (25 cm) aft of the intake. To suit the F110 for

The designation 'Super Tomcat' applied to the F101 DFE testbed aircraft was unofficial, and will not be adopted for the planned F-14D
(Grumman)

Tomcat, the forward mounting was lowered and repositioned to mate with the TF30 pick-up points on the fuselage.

The TF30 used an airframe-mounted accessory gearbox, but the F110 has an integral unit, plus digital electronic controls. The latter eliminates the need for engine trimming, a process which often involves flight deck personnel having to reposition parked F-14As on a carrier deck so that the aircraft being worked on can have its engine nozzles pointed out over the side of the deck so that the engines may be run.

Installation of the F110 involves a minimum of structural changes to the airframe, none of which involve primary structure. The nacelle deck frames and inboard side beam stiffeners require trimming, while the gaps between the new afterburner nozzle and the aft fuselage sponson and cantrebody must be filled. The existing inlet and ducting can handle the airflow to the new engine, changes being restricted to altering the ramp scheduling.

Introduction of the F110 involves installing several items of new equipment—an air-turbine starter, integrated drive generator, ram-air turbine, cockpit-mounted engine instruments, plus small items such as new bleed air valves and ball joints. Existing Tomcat systems which must be modified are the environmental control system primary heat exchanger, AICS controller, approach power control, hydraulic pump and cooler, throttle, and fuel cells.

One advantage of the F110 which will be appreciated by maintenance crews is that the blades are designed to permit minor FOD damage to be blended out. This is possible on the existing TF30, but only to a minor degree.

The F110-400 engine ran for the first time in December 1984. The Navy is keen to see the new engine installed in the Tomcat at the earliest possible date, and is not prepared to wait until the F-14D is developed. A Grumman study carried out at the request of the Navy showed that F110 engined aircraft could be delivered as early as the first quarter of 1988, as the Navy decided to order a 1980s equivalent of the F-14B—an aircraft equipped with F-14A avionics and F110 engines. Known as the F-14A(Plus) this will replace the F-14A on the Grumman line from the spring of 1988 until the first quarter of 1990, the target date for the first F-14D deliveries.

The F-14A avionics are largely analogue, but the F-14D will be a 'digital ship' based on a multiprocessor MIL-STD-1553B database system to which all the avionics systems will be connected. The MIL-STD-1553B databus was devised by the USAF, and was soon adopted by the US Navy and US Army. It is also used by America's allies, often under a different designation. NATO refers to it as STABAG 3838, while the British designation is DEF STAN 00-18 Pt 2. Specification STD-1553B defines a data highway made of simple 'twisted-pair' screened electrical cable to which all the individual avionics systems may be connected. This acts as an 'electronic mail' system, passing data and commands from one unit to another. The data highway replaces much of the maze of electrical cabling and connectors which lie beneath the skin of a modern aircraft, warship or other weapon platform.

The flow of data between subunits is controlled by a small computer known as the bus controller. To avoid the system being knocked out by combat damage, two databuses and two bus controllers are normally used, while each bus consists of two separate twisted pairs routed differently.

In the case of the F-14D, the controllers—

Installation of the F101 DFE engine in the No 7 prototype. The aircraft was later reworked as the first F110-powered F-14D
(Grumman)

designated Mission Computers 1 and 2—will be a pair of the US Navy's standard AYK-14 computers, one being connected to each databus. Mean time between failure of the computer is 2200 hours, and in the F-14D arrangements have been made for one to take over the functions of the other in the event of a failure.

The AYK-14 Standard Airborne Computer is, as its name suggests, a widely used item of data-processing equipment. Already adopted for the F/A-18A Hornet, AV-8B Harrier II, EA-6B Prowler, E-2C Hawkeye, P-3C and EP-3 versions of Orion, and the SH-60 LAMPS Mk 3 helicopter. The production run could reach 10,000 or more. Compatible with the UYK-60—standard microcomputer of the US Navy—it is a general-purpose digital computer suitable for airborne applications, and will easily interface with shipboard and shore-based UYK-60-based equipments. Within the next few years the AYK-14 will be upgraded by the application of Very High Speed Integrated Circuit (VHSIC) devices, the improved version being fielded before the end of the decade.

Current production models of the F-14A are being

delivered with the Block IV model of the AWG-9 radar. The US Navy awarded Hughes a contract to develop the Block V version complete with a Programmable Signal Processor (PSP). This digitized the signal processing within the AWG-9; the current radar is digital, but relies on analogue signal processing. A technical evaluation was completed, showing the advantages of the digitized set, but no production order followed. AWG-9 Block V would have used Schottky electronic-technology components, but the emerging gate-array technology held a clear promise of processors combining greater memory size and faster processing speeds—features which could be used to give a radar better ECCM performance and growth capability.

When the F-14D programme was launched, Hughes was working on the Multi-Staged Improvement Program (MSIP) radar for the F-15 Eagle, a set which used gate-array electronics, so the way was clear to apply this technology to the Tomcat. The resulting radar retains only four weapon-replaceable assemblies (WRAs) of the AWG-9 in their original form, and a further four in modified form. No less than 14 WRAs are deleted, being replaced by nine new units. Some WRAs of the new set (the analogue signal converter, radar signal processor and radar data processor) use the new Schottky technology, and have high commonality with the equivalent sections of the F-15 MSIP radar.

In view of these drastic modifications, the set will no longer be designated AWG-9, but will receive a designation in the APG series. For planning purposes it was known as the APG-XX. On the F-14A integration of the missiles is handled by the AWG-9, but on the -14D this is done by the stores-management system, thus the set joins the APG series of radar designations rather than the AWG series of weapons-control systems. On the current AWG-9, Hughes has worked with Grumman as an associate contractor, but for development and initial production of the APG-XX it will be a subcontractor.

Features of the new set include a low-sidelobe

Altitude testing of the F110 engine at the Arnold Engineering and Development Center, Tullahoma, Tennessee. Based on the F101 engine of the B-1, and originally known as the F101 DFE (General Electric)

ABOVE
High speed subsonic test flight of the F101 DFE testbed
(Grumman)

OPPOSITE PAGE
Conversion of the F-14B into a F101 DFE testbed was
relatively simple, but the aircraft is being more extensively
modified for its new role as the first F110-powered F-14D
prototype
(Grumman)

antenna, a sidelobe-blanking guard channel, and monopulse angle tracking (all of which should make the radar less vulnerable to jamming), plus digital scan control. Currently the AWG-9 has a two-second 'frame time'—the volume being scanned must be covered every two seconds. This requirement is dictated by the need to illuminate missiles in flight during multi-shot engagements. Instead of the two and four-bar scan patterns currently used for this purpose, the new radar's digital scan control allows the set to depart from fixed scan patterns and concentrate part of its attention on other areas of high importance.

The set also incorporates target-identification technology. This is highly-classified, but is largely a matter of analyzing the radar signature of the target in order to identify the type of aircraft being tracked. Inputs from ESM and non-radar sensors will probably also play some part in this difficult task.

A key feature of the avionics improvement in the F-14D is the use of kit developed under several DoD programmes aimed at developing equipment for use in a range of tactical aircraft. Equipment of this type includes the JTIDS, the ASPJ Infra-Red Search and

Track Set (IRST), and the AIM-120A AMRAAM missile. The US Navy also demanded that the F-14D have maximum avionics commonality with aircraft it will serve alongside—the F/A-18 Hornet and the updated A-6E.

The Infra-Red Search and Track (IRST) sensor will supplement rather than replace the Northop AXX-1 TCS TV sensor. The two sensor will probably share a single dual-role chin fairing. Competitive designs for IRST are being developed by General Electric and ITT. Both use a focal-plane IR detector and complex signal processing to overcome the performance deficiencies traditionally associated with IR trackers.

Radar-warning receiver for the F-14D is the Itek ALR-67, which incorporates both the traditional crystal-video pattern of receiver used for radar warning, plus a superheterodyne receiver controlled by a high-speed reprogrammable digital processor. Earlier RWRs were hard-wired and thus relatively inflexible in the face of an evolving threat.

Development of the ALR-67 is continuing. Under Program PE 64225N a new receiver is being designed to increase covering into millimetre-wave and laser frequencies. Other modifications will upgrade receiver performance to cope with the higher signal densities anticipated in the 1990s.

The ALQ-165 Advanced Self-Protection Jammer (ASPJ) being developed for the USAF and US Navy and planned for installation in the F-14D is the most ambitious and expensive current US EW programme. The price tag for equipping a single aircraft with the system is around $1.0 million, and the entire development and production bill could exceed $4 billion. It is expected to serve on most US fighter aircraft until the next century.

R&D started in the summer of 1969, and some of the technology needed was drawn from earlier projects such as the USAF's Risk Reduction Program and ALQ-131 jamming pod, and USN work on wide-band dual-mode countermeasures. In September 1979, rival ITT/Westinghouse and Northrop/Sanders teams were given development contacts, with the former being selected to move into full development.

Prototypes were delivered to the US Navy in FY83, and testing of the vital Comprehensive Power Management System followed soon after. The first full-scale development system was delivered to General Dynamics in January 1984. Initial flight testing of the ALQ-165 was due to begin in 1985, first on an F-16C Fighting Falcon, later on an F/A-18A Hornet. In USN service ALQ-165 will be integrated with the ALR-67 RWR, a task which is being carried out using the F/A-18 as a testbed. In addition to the F-14D, it will also be fitted to the F-15 Eagle. It may also be retrofitted into A-6 aircraft and added in pod-mounted form to the F-14A and AV-8B.

The problems of packing such a complex system within the available weight and volume limits posed a great challenge to the design team, but were quickly overcome. Other aspects of the programme were less easy, however. Rising cost, coupled with technical difficulties caused the US Navy to delay production of the system until FY86, and to fix a cost ceiling.

Like all EW systems, ALQ-165 will need to be updated throughout its lifetime in order to match the evolving threat. Improvements planned under Project W1728 include the development of smaller antennas, high-speed reprogrammable memory, and facilities to allow system software to be reprogrammed in operational service. ALQ-165 will eventually be replaced by the even more sophisticated INEWS EW suite currently in the early stages of development and tipped to serve on the USAF's F-19 Stealth Fighter and Advanced Technology Bomber.

For navigation, the F-14D will be fitted with the ASN-130 digital inertial navigation system. Also used by the F/A-18A, it will also form part of the A-6E upgrade. The new ASN-139 laser inertial navigation system (LINS) is being designed to be form, fit and function compatible with the -130, and may be adopted by the Navy at a later date. The Standard Attitude Heading Reference System (SAHRS) is another common avionics item, and is also due to be fitted to the A-6E.

The stores-management system of the F-14D is based on that of the F/A-18. The processor which forms the heart of the system has a high commonality with the F/A-18 system, but has been modified to handle stores unique to the Tomcat such as Phoenix, and to delete the unrequired air-to-ground modes.

For communications, the F-14D will be fitted with one of the most important items of multi-service electronics currently being developed in the USA. The Joint Tactical Information Distribution System (JTIDS) is an integrated communications, navigation, and identification system intended to provide secure jam-resistant voice and digital data communications, and precision navigation facilities. Intended for naval, air, and ground use, it will be available in several forms. Class 1 command terminals will be installed on USN warships which have a major command and control function—aircraft carriers, cruisers, and amphibious command and control ships. Class 1A terminals are primarily intended for use in airborne early warning (AEW) aircraft such as the Grumman E-2C Hawkeye. Smallest and cheapest of all is the Class 2 terminal, more than 1800 of which will be needed for use in tactical aircraft and smaller warships such as frigates. 'Cheap' is not a word to be used lightly when discussing a unit costing almost $200,000, but purchase of a single Class 1 unit would leave little change from $500,000.

The F-14D pilot will have a HUD, plus three multi-function head-down displays used for vertical situation, horizontal situation and EW data. The RIO will have a new digital data radar display, the Tactical Information display from the F-14A, and two multi-function displays used for horizontal information and EW data. The cockpit-mounted multifunction displays are of the type used in the F/A-18A. The Hornet HUD would not physically fit within the F-14 cockpit, so a new low-profile unit had to be designed. This is not of the recently-developed wide-angle type, since the heavy windscreen prevented a similar installation. In keeping with the USN desire for commonality, the new HUD will also be used in the A-6E update programme. The cockpit displays are all programmable units, physically identical to their F/A-18 equivalents but reprogrammed for the Tomcat role.

One significant difference between the F-14D displays and the F/A-18A installation is that the Hornet avionics designers opted to include low-level data processing—tasks such as writing symbology on the screen—in the aircraft's main AYK-14 computers. For Tomcat, much of this mundane work is done by separate processors distributed around the system, reducing the demands being made on the

A USN F-5E trainer—a type used to simulate the MiG-21 during dissimilar air combat training—tucks in close behind the F101 DFE testbed
(Grumman)

databuses and AYK-14s. The system will be able to automatically re-configure itself in real time in the event of equipment failure or combat damage, informing the crew how much system performance has been degraded.

Also interfaced with the databus system will be engine monitoring system. Designed to observe critical engine parameters, this will allow groundcrews to carry out 'on-condition' maintenance, servicing the F110 as required rather than on a pre-arranged schedule. This will reduce the amount of work to be done by USN technicians, and avoid the wear and tear caused by unnecessary dismantling.

Long-range firepower of the F-14D is provided by a derivative of the AIM-54C, the AIM-54C (Sealed). The AIM-54A and AIM-54C are liquid cooled, and rely on a flow of coolant from the parent aircraft. This passes through the weapon, then returns to the aircraft to lose the heat which it has picked up. As might be imagined, this system presents maintenance problems. The umbilicals sometimes develop leaks, or the cooling oil becomes contaminated. The AIM-54C (Sealed) will have a built-in closed cycle cooling system, and will not exchange coolant with the

aircraft. As part of the development work on this project, Hughes was awarded $4.8 million contract in November 1984 to modify and instrument with thermal sensors five Phoenix missiles which the company will flight test.

F-14D will be able to fire existing AIM-54A and AIM-54C missiles. The older weapon will fit onto the F-14D Phoenix hardpoints but these will not have the facility to supply the weapons with coolant. There are therefore some performance restrictions on the aircraft when carrying AIM-54A in order to minimize aerodynamic heating effects. Minor systems differences also exist between the old and new missiles, but the F-14D can cope with these.

Hughes has proposed a new Phoenix variant designated AIM-54X and designed to match the full potential range of the AWG-9 radar, but preliminary planning for a new long range missile is already under way in order to match the threats postulated for the 1990s. This would be a smaller and higher-speed missile powered by a solid-propellant ducted ram-jet and having a similar range and capability to the AIM-54C. Despite such studies, Phoenix will be Tomcat's primary long-range punch until the end of the decade.

Planned replacement for Sparrow is the Hughes AIM-120A Advanced Medium-Range Air-to-Air Missile (AMRAAM), a technically innovative missile intended to offer most of the performance of the

Sparrow in a weapon not much larger than Sidewinder. Designed to cope with the threats likely to be fielded between now and the late 1990s, this offers fire-and-forget performance and the ability to carry out all-weather attacks from any approach angle and at both visual and beyond-visual ranges.

The AIM-120 is smaller and lighter than the AIM-7 it will replace. AMRAAM is 140.7 inches (357 cm) long, 7 inches (18 cm) in diameter and 20.7 inch (53 cm) in wingspan. Although similar in general configuration to Sparrow, it is smaller and lighter, weighting only 327 lb (148 kg). Unlike Sparrow, it has Phoenix-style fixed wings and moveable tail surfaces. The latter are moved by electrical actuators rather than the hydraulic actuators used in most current weapons.

A dual-mode guidance system allows up to six rounds to be launched against multiple targets between 30 and 40 nm (55–75 km) away. For the first part of the flight to the target, the missile is guided by an inertial reference unit programmed before launch with details of target position. During long-range engagements, the launch aircraft will transmit updated target data to the missile, correcting the inertially-guided trajectory. Once close to the predicted target location, the missile's active-radar seeker is energized. Once the target has been acquired, final homing is automatic, requiring no co-operation from the launch aircraft. AMRAAM is thus a true 'fire-and-forget' missile. A 'home-on-jam' operating mode is also available. The blast/fragmentation warhead weighs 48 lb (22 kg) and is triggered by a proximity fuze.

These ambitious performance goals were originally coupled with equally demanding cost targets—the price tag of an AMRAAM missile was originally set at around $110,000—half that of Sparrow and not much more than that of the AIM-9 Sidewinder. By 1983, the US General Accounting Office (GAO) had already estimated total programme cost at $4,000 million.

The new radar in the F-14D will be matched by new rear-cockpit consoles. These use digital electronics and have a bigger and brighter display, plus computer-style keyboard with software reprogrammable switches (Grumman)

The US Navy has a requirement for 7,000 AMRAAMs for service on the F-14 (which can carry 2, 4 or 8 rounds), and on the F/A-18 (8 or 10 rounds). The USAF order would be for 13,000 to arm the F-115 (8 rounds) and F-16 (4 or 8 rounds). It is also due to be fitted to Allied aircraft, the first probably being the British Aerospace Sea Harrier which is scheduled to receive the weapon in 1986 as part of a mid-life update.

Raytheon has been selected to act as a second source for the AMRAAM programme; the USAF gave Hughes a $9 million contract in July 1982 to cover the work involved in providing Raytheon with the technical information, hardware and other assistance needed in order to allow a second production line to be set up. The decision was strongly criticized at the time, Hughes having effectively been ordered to hand over its successful design to its largest rival. In the short-term, the production work will be split 60:40, with Hughes receiving the larger share, but once Raytheon has been fully-qualified to build the missile, subsequent orders will be placed according to the result of competitive bidding.

AMRAAM may have the potential to revolutionize air combat, but its effectiveness may be hampered by other factors, giving some of the weapon's features at best marginal usefulness. Long-range missile combat demands reliable target identification, but the current Mk 12 IFF system was designed in the 1950s. Its known inadequacies are such that aircraft so fitted will be unable to make full use of AMRAAM's long range to pick off targets at beyond visual range. There are still no firm plans to field an improved NATO-interoperable IFF system, although replacing the obsolete equipment remains a high USAF priority.

Installation of AMRAAM into the F-14D is covered by an option on the current contract, which the Navy were due to decide on by October 1985. The weapon may not form part of the basic F-14D configuration, but could be introduced later. This

The AIM-54C has been developed primarily for use on the F-14D. Its electronics use the latest microelectronic technology, eliminating the need for a supply of liquid coolant from the launch aircraft (Hughes Aircraft)

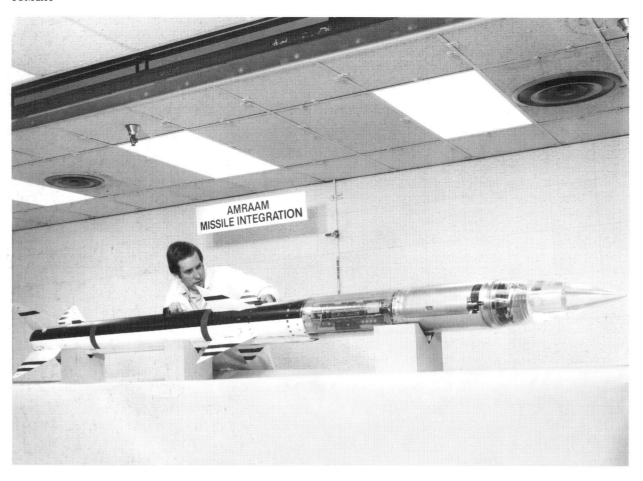

would present no great difficulties, thanks to the multibus system. The addition of AMRAAM would only entail software change.

Following extensive DT&E/IOT&E (Development, Test and Evaluation/Initial Operational Test and Evaluation), test firings of the AIM-120A, initial procurement was to have begun in 1984, but the programme has been hit by a combination of cost and technical problems. The weapon was to have entered operational service in 1986, but this date has now slipped to the summer of 1988. Cost/performance tradeoffs have been studied, and the Pentagon is even considering cancellation. If this happens, a new multi-target version of Sparrow able to engage three or four opponents simultaneously is likely to be developed.

Long-term US medium-range missile plans seem to be based on USAF research work. A new passive/active radar seeker able to provide additional passive operating modes, giving missiles anti-radiation and home-on-jam facilities have been flight tested, along with two possible propulsion systems—a reduced smoke two-pulse rocket motor and a ducted rocket motor.

The Soviet Air Force is taking steps to reduce its vulnerability to heat-seeking missiles. IR flares are being used in massive quantities by strike aircraft operating against Mujahad guerillas in Afghanistan,

The Hughes AIM-120A AMRAAM (Advanced Medium Range Air-to-Air Missile) is a joint USAF/USN replacement for the AIM-7 Sparrow, yet it is only an option for the F-14D. Is the USN resisting the introduction of a weapon which started life as a USAF missile?
(Hughes Aircraft)

and it is reasonable to assume that IR jammers are under development if not in service. This has forced the West to develop improved guidance systems. The dual-waveband Stinger man-portable SAM is being deployed in place of the earlier Redeye, while a new ECM-resistant guidance system is being developed for the Chaparral SAM. Similar development may be expected in the air-to-air field. The Navy is apparently developing a new charge-coupled device (CCD) seeker for Sidewinder.

Tomcat could in theory carry the European developed Advanced Short-Range Air-to-Air Missile (ASRAAM). Covered by the second part of the international MoU which established the AMRAAM as a NATO-standard weapon, ASRAAM is planned to be a lightweight 'dogfighting' missile able to replace existing types such as the AIM-9L Sidewinder. The project is currently being handled by British Aerospace Dynamics (UK) and Bodenseewerk Geratetechnik (West Germany), although France could in theory join the programme at a later date. An agreement between the two partners and Hughes Aircraft calls for the US company to advise on aspects of the ASRAAM programme relevant to US procurement procedures and other factors involved in the purchase of air-to-air missile systems by the US services.

One feature of the armament which could not be changed was the gun. In the absence of a suitable replacement the M61 will have to remain in service. The USAF did try to develop the 25 mm GAU-7 cannon for the F-15, but problems with this weapon and its caseless ammunition resulted in cancellation back in March 1974. Several studies of new guns are currently under way, but all are at an early stage. These include a high velocity gun based on light-gas propellant and offering a muzzle velocity of 8,000 to 10,000 ft/sec (2434 to 3050 m/sec), and novel schemes to steer the fire of a fighter cannon by flexing the barrel. If these prove successful, a retrofit scheme for the F-14D could be considered, since the veteran M61 is hardly an ideal weapon for 1990s air combat.

The only upgrade in this area is therefore the provision of an F/A-18 director type gunsight. The F/A-18 gun sighting system is well liked by pilots, so the same system will be installed on the F-14D to tackle the task of processing the aiming algorithms and generating the appropriate symbology on the HUD.

As this text was being written, aircraft No 7 was on the shop floor at Calverton being modified for its new role as an F-14D propulsion testbed. As part of this upgrade, Grumman is bringing the aircraft up to production standard, carrying out structural modifications such as the installation of revised cowls for the engine bays, redesigned fuel cell liners, a ram-air turbine, and relocated fuel vents to suit the new powerplant. Fatigue cracks resulting from its earlier career were also being repaired. The ram-air turbine will be located in a compartment just forward of the port stabilizer. When deployed, the ram-air turbine swings downwards in the vertical plane, allowing its 7 inch propellor to run up to speed in the slipstream. On aircraft No 7, the compartment used to house the ram-air turbine originally housed a hydrazine-powered starter for the F401 engine. This aircraft will fly in the summer of 1986, and will be used for engine performance testing and envelope-expansion work.

Four F-14s designated PA-1, PA-2, PA-3 and PA-4 will take part in the flight-test programme. Three will be TF30 powered aircraft used for radar, avionics and system testing. Only PA-2 (due to fly in March 1987) will be a true prototype, having the new F110 engine, plus the revised avionics and radar. F-14A No 501 was delivered to the Navy in December 1984 but never saw operational service. Retained at Calverton, it is being rebuilt as PA-1, and will fly just ahead of PA-2 to begin navigation and system function tests. Aircraft 517 was not due for completion until the end of 1985, but is due to be

Test firing of AMRAAM against a QF-102 drone target. Launch aircraft is an F-16, watched by F-4 flying chase (top)
(Hughes Aircraft)

rebuilt as PA-3, flying in the summer of 1987 for radar development and demonstration purposes. It will be closely followed by PA-4 (F-14A No 482), scheduled for weapons and stores-management trials.

Software development will be an immense task, so Grumman will follow an incremental plan, developing this in seven stages. Each will introduce new functions, gradually expanding the performance of the avionics. G1 standard software will be used for initial tests of the radar aboard Hughes' TA-3B Skywarrior testbed. This obsolete twin-engined Douglas attack bomber is big enough to carry the radar and the crew of engineers who will test and troubleshoot. It should begin flying in February 1987, about a month ahead of PA-1 which will have G2 standard software.

All PA-series trials aircraft will start with G2 software, with G3 and G4 being developed in the course of the year. G5 will become available in the spring of 1988, with G6 following in the summer, and the definitive G7 standard being ready by the beginning of 1989. Individual trials aircraft will not necessarily have the same software standard, or

receive the latest standard available. PA-1 will downgrade from G5 to G4 in the summer of 1988 for USN technical evaluations, then jump to G6, while PA-3 will never receive G5, moving directly from G4 to G6. Software will be written in CMS2, the standard US Navy computer language. The F-14D is too early to use ADA, the official DoD computer language for all future projects.

Under current plans, the first batch of 12 F-14D aircraft will be ordered in FY88. The first F-14Ds should be delivered in March 1990, and production is expected to peak at 30 per year. A total of up to 306 F-14D are planned. This will bring the US Navy's total Tomcat buy to a grand total of 899 aircraft at a total cost to the US taxpayer of around $38.9 billion.

Tomcat pilots regard themselves as members of an exclusive club, but the lucky few to have flown F101/F110-powered aircraft form the most exclusive group of all. Until the end of the decade, most Tomcat pilots must be content to nurse their aging TF30s and dream of F110s. Early in 1985, the author visited Grumman to gather the material for this book, and pilot Joe Burke from the company's flight test operation took time to describe the experience of flying the F101-powered No 7 aircraft.

'When you light the afterburner for take-off, you know you've got a different airplane . . . the engines accelerate quicker, it's a smoother operation.' In air combat between equally skilled pilots, a modest performance edge is sufficient to give one the upper hand. 'If the other guy's got a slight performance edge on you, it may take a while, but it will show up. Take two airplanes of the same type, one at a heavy gross weight and the other at a light gross weight, the one with the light gross weight (all other things being equal) will have victory. Now when you're talking

A wingless and finless AMRAAM test round undergoes captive testing under the port wing of a PMTC Tomcat from Point Mugu
(Grumman)

about 35 per cent more thrust, it's going to show up very quickly. It translates into higher sustained turning performance, and being able to manoeuvre in the vertical longer and higher than the other airplane.'

Absence of engine stalls will make a big difference to Tomcat operations. Pilots currently 'fly the engine' and have to spend time monitoring the engines instead of concentrating on the task of flying the aircraft. 'If we can fly the airplane alone, and depend on the engine, that's going to allow the pilot to do more with the airplane—he'll do a better job . . . pilots will be more aggressive.'

In designing the F-14D, Grumman asked the Navy to specify the most common air combat conditions. These turned out to be around Mach 0.9/15,000 ft (4500 m), so the aircraft and its engine were optimized for this part of the performance envelope. For the original F101 DFE flight test programme using prototype No 7, it became obvious that with the new powerplant, the pilot would be free to move the throttles at will without stalling the engine. Smoke emission is low, a useful bonus in air combat, making visual acquisition more difficult.

The lower fuel consumption of the F110 has a significant effect on range, as does the fact that the new engine allows catapult take-offs to be made without the use of afterburner, even when the aircraft is operating at maximum gross weight. With both engines running, the F-14A could take off in dry thrust, but the climb rate would be marginal should an engine fail.

Armed with four Phoenix, two Sparrows and two Sidewinders, the F-14D will be able to loiter 150 nm from the carrier for just over two hours, a 34 per cent improvement over the F-14A. If a one hour CAP loiter is required, the aircraft can fly this 367 nm from the carrier (a 45 per cent improvement over the F-14A). Deck launched intercept ranges with Mach 1.3 and Mach 1.5 flyout rise by an impressive 62 per cent to 277 and 217 nm respectively.

The US Navy is keen to update the F-14A fleet, but has yet to finalize its ideas. It still hopes that modifications to the TF30 will finally produce the desired reliability. P&W has proposed modifying the TF30 at no charge to the Navy and is conducting two improvement programmes for the engine involving increasing durability and operability in the F-14. An improved TF30 is scheduled for introduction in late 1986. If P&W does not manage to improve the TF30, the chances of an F110 retrofit will be increased.

Plans for installation of the GE engine have been studied, plus a various degrees of avionics updating. As this text was being written, it seemed likely that the F110 would be retrofitted to at least part of the F-14A fleet, plus some of the F-14D avionics. Even if an 'engine-only' scheme were to be adopted, this would be unlikely to begin until the end of the decade. The F-14D will be the priority candidate for early-production F110s.

By the end of the decade, the USN plans to have 15 deployable carriers. The 13th—*Carl Vinson*—joined the fleet in FY82, and the next, CVN-71 *Theodore Roosevelt* was launched in 1984, and will join the fleet in FY87. The 15th—CVN-72 *Abraham Lincoln*— will bring the fleet up to strength at the end of the

Despite one and a half decades of operational service, Tomcat still looks more like a futuristic mount for Luke Skywalker and R2D2 than a fighter for service aircrew. Boosted in combat effectiveness by the introduction of the F110 engine, AIM-54C missile and new avionics, it will remain a deadly opponent well into the next century (Grumman)

decade. One more carrier is currently authorized— CVN-72 *George Washington*. This is due for deployment by 1992. *Coral Sea* will then probably be redesignated a training carrier. Under the Service Life Extension Program, each of the first eight post-war carriers (from the *Forrestal* to the *Kennedy*), are being withdrawn one by one for rebuilds of up to two years' duration.

First to undergo this process—which adds a further 15 years to each vessel's original 30 year life— was carried out on the *Saratoga*, followed by *Forrestal*. After *Independence*, *Kitty Hawk* will be next, but an examination of the structure of this carrier suggests that she is in better condition than the previous vessels, and will require less work, allowing a shorter and less expensive SLEP. A study of the other unrenovated carriers is being performed to see if they too might be candidates for shorter reworks. This programme may be expensive, but the USN considers it a very economical alternative to new construction. Under this plan, the USN will not have to build any carriers beyond *George Washington* until the early 1990s, when the *Midway* and the *Forrestal* will probably need replacing. Retirement of the SLEPed carriers will probably begin in the late 1990s with *Midway*, then progressively until *Kennedy* is retired in around 2015.

With the export of MiG-29 *Fulcrum* fighters to India in the summer of 1985, it can only be a matter of time before this advanced aircraft is in worldwide service, so the introduction of the F-14D will be timely. The new aircraft may be a great improvement over the existing F-14A, but Soviet design bureaux are hardly likely to ignore the challenge which it poses, while the Soviet Air Force and Naval Aviation must try to develop new tactics to deal with the upgraded Tomcat.

In a full-scale war, one possible anti-F-14D tactic might be to attempt to overwork its crew by launching repeated air attacks with *Backfire* bombers, forcing Tomcat crews to fly repeated 400–500 mile sorties. Back in 1980 when the Advanced Technology Bomber (ATB) was started, the US Secretary of Defense Harold Brown announced that a study was being carried out to determine whether long-range shore-based aircraft could augment or even replace some carriers. Classified studies have already raised the prospect that under some circumstances land-based aircraft might prove more cost-effective than carriers. The solution to multi-wave air attacks might be to have one or more B-1s armed with long-range ballistic air-intercept missiles on station over the threatened carrier group.

Grumman is already studying post F-14D fighters, carrying out studies of the outer air battle to see what improvements might be useful. One obvious problem will come when the Soviet Union finally fields a Phoenix-class missile, and the US Navy loses its ability to impose attrition on attackers at long range without risk to its own fighters. Two-way air combat at ranges of more than 100 nm will pose tremendous technical difficulties, particularly in the face of the dense ECM environment of the future.

The USAF is already working on its Advanced Tactical Fighter to replace the F-15 Eagle, but there is as yet no real progress on an F-14 replacement for the Navy. The service believes that the F-14D will be able to match the threat until beyond the end of the century. Studies of a new fighter able to replace both the F-14 and the A-6 Intruder began in 1983. Several companies, including General Dynamics, Grumman, McDonnell Douglas, and Rockwell started preliminary studies based on projected threat assessments, attempting to identify the techniques and technologies required to create a suitable aircraft. This VFMX project would have entered full-scale development in the late 1980s, but the decision to field the F-14D and an upgraded Intruder has allowed a degree of slowdown.

Requests for proposals covering concept-definition studies of an Advanced Tactical Aircraft (ATA) were due to be issued in the spring of 1985, but this requirement is focussed on replacing the A-6 Intruder. The possibility of a follow-on intercept variant have been discussed, but with production deliveries not due until 1997, the F-14D seems assured of a long career.

First results of ATA work are still classified but some observers are already predicting an aircraft in the size and weight class of the Tomcat. Assuming this is matched by Tomcat-level costs, affordability and short production runs could be a problem. Barring technological breakthroughs, the days of the cheap naval interceptor seem over.

Perhaps the last word on the subject of Tomcat is best left to Mike Pelehach. 'When we get the new engine in the F-14, I don't think that there's anything that will come close to it, performance-wise. Performance of an airplane is there for one reason, to put the airplane at that point in the sky where the weapon system is optimized, that's really what it's all about. You want to get that airplane at the point that gives you the best chance of downing a particular target. For the airplane to get involved in dogfighting—that's past, it's a joke, its time has come.

'What justifies the F-14 is that it carries six Phoenix missiles—so you really have six kills per airplane. If you have less than that, then you end up with a problem of affordability. If you look at the airplanes we are building today, or talking about building, you are talking in terms of fighter airplanes costing in excess of $15 million. If you had to build airplanes at the rate that we built the F-4 at the end of the Vietnam war—73 a month—the programme would cost $20 billion a year. The United States doesn't have that kind of money, nor does anyone else. Unless you make war with the missiles and systems in the so-called "high-cost" airplanes, you can't afford it. I defy anyone to come up with numbers that are affordable. You're going to have to go to something different, and that's the problem the F-14 is tackling.'

Glossary

AEW	airborne early warning	INS	inertial navigation system
buno	bureau number	LRU	line replaceable unit
CIA	Central Intelligence Agency	MoD	Ministry of Defence
CRT	cathode-ray tube	NASA	National Aeronautics and Space Administration
DoD	Department of Defense		
ECM	electronic counter measures	NAS	Naval Air Station
ECCM	electronic counter-counter measures	NATF	Naval Air Test Facility
EW	electronic warfare	SAM	surface-to-air missile
FBI	Federal Bureau of Investigation	TACAN	Tactical Air Navigation System
IFF	identification friend or foe	TISEO	Target Identification System Electro-Optical

Acknowledgements

The following individuals and organizations are notable among those who have assisted me during the preparation of this book.

Grumman Aerospace
Grumman History Center
Hughes Aircraft
Northrop

Robert F Dorr
Lindsay Peacock
Jean-Pierre Montbazet
Barry C Wheeler

Specifications

F-14A

Type: two-seat carrier-based multi-role fighter

Powerplant: two 20,900 lb (9480 kg) afterburning Pratt & Whitney TF30-414 turbofans

Performance: maximum speed (clean) Mach 2.34 or 2486 km/h at 40,000 ft (12,190 m); cruising speed 400–550 knots (741–1019 km/h); landing speed 132 knots (204 km/h); minimum take-off distance 1,400 ft (427 m); service ceiling over 50,000 ft (15,240 m)

Weights: empty 39,921 lb (18,036 kg); maximum take-off with four AIM-7 59,531 lb (26,931 kg); maximum take-off with six AIM-54 70,599 lb (31,945 kg); maximum internal fuel load 16,200 lb (7127 kg); maximum external fuel load 3784 lb (1720 kg)

Dimensions: wing span (unswept) 64 ft 1½ in (19.55 m); swept 38 ft 2.4 in (11.65 m); overswept for deck parking 33 ft 3½ in (10.15 m); length 62 ft 10.6 in (19.1 m); height 16 ft (4.88 m); wing area 565 sq ft (52.5² m)

Armament: one General Electric M61A1 Vulcan, Gatling-style 20 mm cannon with 675 rounds; provision for six AIM-7F/M Sparrow and four AIM-9L/P Sidewinder AAMs, or six AIM-54A/C Phoenix and two AIM-9L/P AAMs, or four AIM-54A/C, two AIM-7F/M, and two AIM-9L/P AAMs

(Notes: F-14B powered by two 28,096 lb (12,745 kg) afterburning Pratt & Whitney F401-PW-400 turbofans; first flight 12 September 1973 but no production. F-14D will be powered by two 28,000 lb (12,727 kg) General Electric F110-GE-400 afterburning turbofans).

Appendices

Appendix I. F-14 Tomcats Manufactured

Model	Amount	From	To	Remarks
F-14A-01-GR	1	157980	—	FY69
F-14A-05-GR	1	157981	—	FY 69
F-14A-10-GR	1	157982	—	FY 69
F-14A-15-GR	1	157983	—	FY 69
F-14A-20-GR	1	157984	—	FY 69
F-14A-25-GR	1	157985	—	FY 70
F-14A-30-GR	1	157986	—	FY 70
F-14A-35-GR	1	157987	—	FY 70
F-14A-40-GR	1	157988	—	FY 70
F-14A-45-GR	1	157989	—	FY 70
F-14A-50-GR	1	157990	—	FY 70
F-14A-55-GR	1	157991	—	FY 69
F-14A-60-GR	8	158612	158619	FY 71
F-14A-65-GR	18	158620	158637	FY 71
F-14A-70-GR	29	158978	159006	FY 72
F-14A-75-GR	19	159007	159025	FY 72
F-14A-75-GR	9	159421	159429	FY 73
F-14A-80-GR	39	159430	159468	FY 73
F-14A-85-GR	50	159588	159637	FY 74
F-14A-90-GR	50	159825	159874	FY 75
F-14A-GR	30	160299	160328	Iran (3-863/3-892)
F-14A-GR	50	160329	160378	Iran (3-893/3-942)
F-14A-95-GR	36	160379	160414	FY 76
F-14A-100-GR	45	160652	160696	FY 77
F-14A-105-GR	44	160887	160930	FY 78
F-14A-110-GR	36	161133	161168	FY 79
F-14A-115-GR	30	161270	161299	FY 80
F-14A-120-GR	30	161416	161445	Fy 81
F-14A-125-GR	30	161597	161626	FY 82
F-14A-130-GR	30	161850	161879	FY 83
F-14A-135-GR	24	162588	162611	FY 84
F-14A-140-GR	24	162612	162638	FY 85
Total to date	643			

Appendix 2. **US Navy F-14A Tomcat Squadrons**

I. Atlantic Fleet

Squadron	Nickname	Traditional Home Port
VF-11	Red Rippers	NAS Oceana, Virginia
VF-14	Tophatters	
VF-31	Tomcatters	
VF-32	Swordsmen	
VF-33	Tarsiers	
VF-41	Black Aces	
VF-74	Bedevilers	
VF-84	Jolly Rogers	
VF-101	Grim Reapers (Training Unit)	
VF-102	Diamondbacks	
VF-103	Sluggers	
VF-142	Ghostriders	
VF-143	The World Famous Pukin' Dogs	

II. Pacific Fleet

Squadron	Nickname	Traditional Home Port
VF-1	Wolfpack	NAS Mirimar, California
VF-2	Bounty Hunters	
VF-21	Freelancers	
VF-24	Fighting Renegades	
VF-51	Screaming Eagles	
VF-111	Sundowners	
VF-114	Aardvarks	
VF-124	Gunfighters (Training Unit)	
VF-154	Black Knights	
VF-211	Fighting Checkmates	
VF-213	Black Lions	

III. Navy Reserve

VF-301	Devil's Disciples	NAS Mirimar, California
VF-302	Fighting Stallions	

(Note: test unit VX-4 'The Evaluators' at Point Mugu, California, the Naval Air Test Center at Pax River, Maryland, the Strike Aircraft Test Directorate and the Pacific Missile Test Center at Point Mugu, and NASA at Dryden—Edwards AFB, California, also operate the F-14).

Index